Big Data, Big Innovation

Wiley & SAS Business Series

The Wiley & SAS Business Series presents books that help senior-level managers with their critical management decisions.

Titles in the Wiley & SAS Business Series include:

For more information on any of the above titles, please visit www.wiley.com.

Big Data, Big Innovation

Enabling Competitive Differentiation through Business Analytics

Evan Stubbs

WILEY

Published by John Wiley & Sons, Inc., Hoboken, New Jersey.
Published simultaneously in Canada.

For general information on our other products and services or for technical support, please contact our Customer Care Department within the United States at (800) 762-2974, outside the United States at (317) 572-3993 or fax (317) 572-4002.

Wiley publishes in a variety of print and electronic formats and by print-on-demand. Some material included with standard print versions of this book may not be included in e-books or in print-on-demand. If this book refers to media such as a CD or DVD that is not included in the version you purchased, you may download this material at http://booksupport.wiley.com. For more information about Wiley products, visit www.wiley.com.

Library of Congress Cataloging-in-Publication Data:

Stubbs, Evan.
    Big data, big innovation : enabling competitive differentiation through business analytics / Evan Stubbs.
        pages   cm. — (Wiley & SAS business series)
    ISBN 978-1-118-72464-4 (hardback) — ISBN 978-1-118-92553-9 (epdf) — ISBN 978-1-118-92552-2 (epub) — ISBN 978-1-118-91498-4 (obook)
        1. Business planning.   2. Strategic planning.   3. Big data.
    4. Decision making—Statistical methods.   5. Industrial management—Statistical methods.   I. Title.
    HD30.28.S784   2014
    658.4′013—dc23
                                                                    2014007690

Printed in the United States of America

10 9 8 7 6 5 4 3 2 1

Contents

Preface

Writing is an interesting pursuit; where you start is rarely where you end up. This is my third book and while not originally intended to be a trilogy, things seemed to have panned out that way.

My first book, *The Value of Business Analytics*, was written for the "doers," the people responsible for making things happen. It tried to answer the fundamental question people kept asking me: "Why don't people *get* this?"

My second book, *Delivering Business Analytics*, was written for the "designers," the people responsible for working out how things should happen. It opened the kimono, provided solutions to 24 common organizational problems, and laid the framework to identify and replicate best practices. It tried to answer the next question people kept asking me: "I know what I need to do, but *how* do I do it?"

This book is written for the "decision makers" and aims to answer the final question: "How do I innovate?"

There are countless models out there. Many are useful, including the ones presented in this book. Most try to make everyone follow the same approach. However, business analytics works best when it's unique to the organization that leverages it. Differentiation means being different, something that's all too often overlooked. Rather than just trying to copy, I hope you use the models in this book to create your own source of innovation.

I hope you find as much enjoyment reading this book as I had writing it.

Things move quickly. There's always more case studies, more disruption, and more examples of how business analytics is fueling innovation. For the latest, keep the conversation going at http://evanstubbs.com/go/blog.

HOW TO READ THIS BOOK

This book introduces eight models:

1. The **Cultural Imperative**: Covered in Chapter 3, this outlines the five perspectives that support a high-functioning culture.

2. The **Intelligent Enterprise**: Covered in Chapter 4, this explains how organizations build the capability they need to innovate.

3. The **Value of Business Analytics**: Covered in Chapter 6, this explains the value that business analytics creates.

4. The **Wheel of Value**: Covered in Chapter 6, this explains how to get organizations to create value from big data.

5. The **Path to Profitability**: Covered in Chapter 7, this explains how to blend data science with value creation.

6. The **SMART Model**: Covered in Chapter 7, this explains how to hire and develop the right people.

7. The **Value Architect**: Covered in Chapter 7, this explains how to make sure data scientists create value.

8. The **Innovation Engine**: Covered in Chapter 8, this explains how to support innovation through dynamic value.

Everything else in this book outlines, justifies, and explains the steps necessary to make innovation from big data real. Chapter 8 is written for leaders interested in enabling ability and innovation and is arguably the most important chapter to read.

Due to the nature of the subject matter, this book covers a great deal of ground. To keep the content digestible, much of the detail has been summarized; for those interested in more, I'd strongly recommend reading my prior books, *The Value of Business Analytics* and *Delivering Business Analytics*. Where relevant, specific references are provided within the text. Endnotes to further reading are also provided throughout. Rather than a definitive list of reading material, readers should view these as a launching pad from which they can further explore whatever they're interested in.

This book is divided into four parts. The first highlights a number of current and emerging trends that will continue to dramatically change the face of business. It's true that things always change; in the famous words of Benjamin Franklin (among others), "In this world nothing can be said to be certain, except death and taxes." It's also true, however, that we become so accustomed to change that we run the risk of underestimating the enormous disruption caused by continuous gradual change. If big data is the question, business analytics is the solution. Unfortunately for some, the answer it implies will eventually see entire industries disrupted.

The second part provides a framework through which leaders can understand the challenges they're likely to face in changing their organization's culture. It outlines the different perspectives organizations exhibit in moving from unstructured chaos to becoming an intelligent enterprise.

The third part focuses on how to leverage big data to support innovation. This isn't easy. Innovation is amorphous. Business analytics is complex. Big data is daunting. Together, they can seem insurmountable. Within this part, we review the fundamentals behind success. It spans culture, human capital, organizational structure, technology design, and operating models.

Finally, the fourth part links them all into an integrated operating model that covers ideation, innovation, and commercialization; it gives a starting framework to develop a plan. It highlights the major considerations that need to be made and provides some recommendations to ensure that you "stay the course."

As with my other books, this one relies heavily on practical examples throughout. Theory is good but where practice and theory contradict, practice grabs theory by the ears and smashes its head into the canvas. While anyone interested in the topic will hopefully find value in the entire book, readers interested in specific topics will benefit from going to specific sections.

Readers interested in understanding the broader impacts of big data along with how organizations tend to cope with disruption are encouraged to read Parts One and Two.

Readers responsible for restructuring organizations to take advantage of business analytics along with hiring and developing the right people are encouraged to read Parts Two and Three.

Finally, readers interested in integrating these building blocks into an operating model that supports innovation will find Part Four especially valuable.

CORE CONCEPTS

This section presents the core vocabulary for everything discussed in this book. It is provided to ensure consistency with my prior two books as well as to provide a quick primer to newcomers. Readers comfortable with the field are encouraged to skip this section.

This book refers repeatedly to a variety of concepts. While the terms and concepts defined in this chapter serve as a useful taxonomy, they should not be read as a comprehensive list of strict definitions. Depending on context and industry, they may go by other names. One of the challenges of a relatively young discipline such as business analytics is that while there's tremendous potential for innovation, it has yet to develop a standard vocabulary.

Their intent is simply to provide consistency. Terms vary from person to person and while readers may not always agree with the semantics presented here given their own background and context, it's essential that they understand what is meant within this book by a particular word. Key terms are italicized to try to aid readability.

Business analytics is the use of data-driven insight to generate value. It does so by requiring business relevancy, the use of actionable insight, and performance measurement and value measurement.

This can be contrasted against *analytics*, the process of generating insight from data. Analytics without business analytics creates no return—it simply answers questions. Within this book, analytics represents a wide spectrum that covers all forms of data-driven insight, including:

- Data manipulation
- Reporting and business intelligence
- Advanced analytics (including data mining, optimization, and forecasting)

Broadly speaking, analytics divides relatively neatly into techniques that help understand *what happened* and those that help understand:

- What will happen
- Why it happened
- What is the best one could possibly do

Forms of analytics that help provide this greater level of insight are often referred to as *advanced analytics*.

The final output of business analytics is *value* of some form, either *internal* or *external*. Additionally, this book introduces the concept of *dynamic value*, the potential of multiple competing points of view to fuel innovation. Internal value is value as seen from the perspective of a team within the organization. Among other things, returns are usually associated with cost reductions, resource efficiencies, or other internally related financial aspects. External value is value as seen from outside the organization. Returns are usually associated with revenue growth, positive outcomes, or other market- and client-related measures.

This value is created through leveraging *people*, *process*, *data*, and *technology*. Encompassing all of these is *culture*, the shared values and priorities of an organization. *People* are the individuals and their skills involved in applying business analytics. *Processes* are a series of *activities* linked to achieve an outcome and can be either *strongly defined* or *weakly defined*. A strongly defined process has a series of specific steps that is repeatable and can be automated. A weakly defined process, by contrast, is undefined and relies on the ingenuity and skill of the person executing the process to complete it successfully.

Data are quantifiable measures stored and available for analysis. They often include transactional records, customer records, and free-text information such as case notes or reports. *Assets* are produced as an intermediary step to achieving value. Assets are a general class of items that can be defined, are measurable, and have implicit tangible or intangible value. Among other things, they include documented processes, reports, models, and datamarts. Critically, they are only an asset within this book if they can be automated and can be repeatedly used by individuals other than those who created it.

Assets are developed through having a team apply various *competencies*. A competency is a particular set of skills that can be applied to solve a variety of different business problems. Examples include the ability to develop predictive models, the ability to create insightful reports, and the ability to operationalize insight through effective use of technology.

Competencies are applied using various *tools* (often referred to as *technology*) to generate new assets. Often, tools are consolidated into a common *analytical platform*, a technology environment that ranges from being spread across multiple desktop PCs right through to a truly enterprise platform.

Analytical platforms, when properly implemented, make a distinction between a *discovery environment* and an *operational environment*. The role of the discovery environment is to generate insight. The role of the operational environment, by contrast, is to allow this insight to be applied automatically with strict requirements around reliability, performance, availability, and scalability.

The core concepts of people, process, data, technology, and culture feature heavily in this book; while they are a heavily used and abused framework, they represent the core of systems design. Business analytics is primarily about facilitating change; business analytics is nothing without driving towards better outcomes. And, when it comes to driving change, every roadmap involves having an impact across these four dimensions. While this book isn't explicitly written to fit with this framework, it relies heavily on it.

Readers interested in knowing more are heavily encouraged to read *The Value of Business Analytics* and *Delivering Business Analytics*.

Acknowledgments

There were many who provided valuable input and feedback throughout my writing, far too many to acknowledge exhaustively. Their advice was excellent and any mistakes contained inside these pages are solely mine. I would especially like to thank Philip Reschke, Chami Akmeemana, Vicki Batten, Lynette Clunies-Ross, Dorothy Adams, Greg Wood, and Renée Nocker.

Most important of all, I'd like to thank my family. Without their patience, support, and constant caring this would have been impossible. I promise this is the last one—for now.

PART
ONE

May You Live in
Interesting Times

The Chinese have an idiom. Loosely translated, it says that it's better to be a dog in a peaceful time than a man in a chaotic time. There's also a related curse, also often attributed to the Chinese: "May you live in interesting times."

This, in a snapshot, is our world. Our time is one where drones can assassinate someone half-way around the globe, controlled by people on a TV screen from the safety of their own suburb. This is a time where a tiny failed bank in Greece can potentially bring the entire global financial system to a screeching halt, bankrupting nations. It is a time where one can carry the entire Library of Congress on a chip smaller than one's fingernail and still have storage to spare. And it is a time where cars drive themselves, glasses contain computers, and 3D printers can create duplicates of themselves.

We live in interesting times. And, interesting times call for interesting leaders.

CHAPTER 1

Lead or Get Out of the Way

The greatest leaders are as much a product of their time as they are a reflection of their skill. Without Hitler, what would we remember of Churchill? Without Xerxes, the legend of the 300 Spartans led by Leonidas would never have happened. Without the right context, even those with the greatest potential remain part of the peanut gallery, shouting epitaphs at those who wear the limelight.

It's in times of crisis that leaders emerge—times of change, times like the present.

THE FUTURE IS NOW

Our world is a fascinating one; we're at an inflection point, one defined by big data and business analytics. What was once science fiction is becoming reality. Let's be frank though—that sounds pretty hackneyed. After all, hasn't *everything* been science fiction once?

This is true. It's also true, however, that science fiction is a deep well to draw from. A well where some ideas are so fantastical that it seems impossible that they'll ever become reality. Asimov, a science fiction writer, for example, wrote speculatively of "psychohistory" in his *Foundation* series.[1] A form of mathematical sociology, scientists would use massive amounts of behavioral information to predict the future.

Through doing so, they were able to foresee the rise and fall of empires thousands of years in advance.

As with all good stories, power always comes with constraints. Accurate predictions were only possible given two conditions. First, the population whose behaviors were to be modeled needed to be sufficiently large—too small, and the predictions would become error-prone. Second, the population being modeled could not know it was being modeled. After all, people might change what they were doing if they knew they were being watched.

It seems fantastical, doesn't it? Still, this is fundamentally the promise of big data. We know more about the world than ever before. Many of those being watched are still unaware of how much things have changed. Between national intelligence, security leaks, and the potential of metadata, most of us are only just realizing *how much* information is out there. And, by analyzing that data, we have the power to predict the future in ways that people still can't believe. Amazon, for example, took out a patent in late 2013 on a process to ship your goods *before* you've ordered them.[2] Big data offers unparalleled insights and predictive abilities, but only to those who know how to leverage it. For most, getting value from big data is a challenge. However, the reflection of every challenge is opportunity.

Things have changed. And, it's a rare leader who isn't aware he or she needs a plan to realize this opportunity. However, there's a twist. It's not just a good idea. It's not something that's *going* to happen. It's happening *now*.

Catalyzed by books such as *Thinking, Fast and Slow*[3] and *Nudge*,[4] behavioral economics is already blending data with heuristics and psychology to create new models to describe and influence consumer behavior. Recognizing the power of a scientific approach to analyzing information, the U.K. government established a dedicated Behavioral Insights team to take advantage of these ideas. Formed in 2010 and nicknamed the "nudge unit," their goal was to blend quantitative and qualitative techniques to improve policy design and delivery.[5]

The model has proved to be a popular one. In late 2012, the Behavioral Insights Team went global through partnership with the government of New South Wales in Australia. In mid-2013, the Obama administration appointed Yale graduate Maya Shankar to create a similar task force.

Paul Krugman, winner of the Nobel Memorial Prize for Economic Sciences, credits Asimov's vision of a mathematical sociology as inspiring him to enter economics.[6] This vision of a future shaped by our ability to analyze information is becoming real. And, it's changing the face of medicine, policy, and business. Thanks to constantly increasing analytical horsepower and falling storage costs, the cost of sequencing the genome has dropped from US$100 million in 2001 to just over US$8,000 in 2013.[7] More than just being cheaper, every decline in sequencing costs puts us that much closer to truly personalized medicine.

Even the social web is sparking innovation. Facebook's acquisition of Oculus, Instagram, and Whatsapp wasn't just an attempt to diversify. It was a deliberate attempt to stay engaged across all channels *all the time*. With over a billion people now on Facebook, it's amazing what one can find by scanning personal interactions. Organizations like the United Nations (UN) are tracking disease and unemployment in real time through the large-scale analysis of social media.[8] The Advanced Computing Center at the University of Vermont is using tens of millions of geolocated tweets in its Hedonometer project to map happiness levels in cities across the United States.[9]

The future is closer than it's ever been. Taking the leap to Asimov's psychohistory isn't as far-fetched as it once might have seemed.

THE SECRET IS LEADERSHIP

It's hard to ignore the potential of big data. Realizing it, though, that's tricky. For every successful project there's a mountain of failed projects. Few in the field have escaped completely unscathed. Anyone who says she has probably hasn't been trying hard enough.

If you're reading this book, it's a fair assumption that you're interested in linking big data to innovation. The cornerstone to this is business analytics. Big data and business analytics go together hand in glove. Without data, there can be no analysis. And without business analytics, big data is just noise. Together, they offer the potential for innovation. Innovation, however, requires change, and change is impossible without leadership.

Without value, all of this is meaningless. Big data has the potential to make things more efficient. It can generate returns. It might simply answer "the hard questions" that no one knows the solution to. Some of these benefits lead to internal value, such as productivity. Others lead to external value, such as revenue. Still others can lead to total reinvention through dynamic change. Not all of these are complementary. Because of this, harnessing the full potential of big data involves walking the tightrope between the dynamism of change and the stability of continuous improvement.

The secret behind success is leadership. Without it, it's impossible to balance the opportunity for reinvention with the benefits of continual improvement. A strong leader can do more with access to limited capability than the best team can without a leader.

We don't yet know the final impact of big data and business analytics. We do know, however, that it *will* change things. Change in itself isn't new; we already live in a world where change has become so normal that it's almost invisible. However, for reasons that are covered in the next chapter, big data is "bigger" than this. It's likely to cause large-scale industrial and social disruption not seen since the industrial revolution, not because of what it is but because of what it represents.

Our future may be one where the economy only requires a tenth of the current workforce. Guided by the use of operational analytics and intelligent algorithms, it might lead to large-scale social unrest due to chronic unemployment and wealth centralization. It may be one where privacy becomes meaningless and the most personal aspects of our lives become public property. It may be one where *precrime*, the ability to predict crimes before they occur, becomes a reality.[10]

These may seem absurd, but, they're already happening. Through automating analytics, some organizations are able to achieve orders of magnitude of higher levels of productivity than their peers. The impact this will have on the labor market is unclear. Katz, a Harvard economist, suggests that even though there's no precedent for a structural change in the demand for jobs, today's digital technologies present many unanswered questions.[11] Historically, technological innovation has almost always led to greater long-run employment. Thanks to the potential of intelligent systems, the biggest question is this: Will the future reflect the past? It's possible, as far-fetched as it might sound, that the entire middle-skilled strata of the labor market may simply become unemployable.[12]

The division between the "haves" and "have-nots" continues to grow. Sharing selfies and personal details has become the norm on SnapChat, Facebook, and a multitude of other social media sites. Through analyzing interests, social networks, and behavioral patterns, organizations such as Google, LinkedIn, and Facebook have become experts in guessing who you might know. And, some justice departments are already experimenting with predictive analytics to better understand the likelihood of recidivism for offenses such as driving under the influence or domestic violence.

The world doesn't need custodians to navigate this period of rapid change. It needs leaders—people with the confidence, vision, and ability to redefine their world. Whether it's for profit or for the common good, the future is business analytics.

NOTES

1. Isaac Asimov, *Foundation* (Garden City, NY: Doubleday, 1951).
2. U.S. Patent #8,615,473 B2.
3. Daniel Kahneman, *Thinking, Fast and Slow* (New York: Farrar, Straus & Giroux, 2011).
4. Richard H. Thaler and Cass R. Sunstein, *Nudge: Improving Decisions about Health, Wealth, and Happiness* (New Haven, CT: Yale University Press, 2008).
5. Cabinet Office, "Behavioural Insights Team," www.gov.uk/government/organisations/behavioural-insights-team (accessed Jan. 11, 2014).
6. Paul Krugman, "Paul Krugman: Asimov's Foundation Novels Grounded My Economics," *Guardian News and Media*, Dec. 4, 2012, www.theguardian.com/books/2012/dec/04/paul-krugman-asimov-economics (accessed Jan. 11, 2014).
7. National Human Genome Research Institute, "DNA Sequencing Costs," www.genome.gov/sequencingcosts (accessed Jan. 11, 2014).
8. United Nations Global Pulse, www.unglobalpulse.org (accessed Jan. 11, 2014).
9. Hedonometer, "Daily Happiness Averages for Twitter, September 2008 to Present," www.hedonometer.org/index.html (accessed Jan. 11, 2014).
10. Philip K. Dick, *The Minority Report* (New York: Pantheon, 2002).
11. David Rotman, "How Technology Is Destroying Jobs," *MIT Technology Review*, Jun. 12, 2013, www.technologyreview.com/featuredstory/515926/how-technology-is-destroying-jobs (accessed Mar. 27, 2014).
12. "The Onrushing Wave," *Economist* (Jan. 18, 2014), www.economist.com/news/briefing/21594264-previous-technological-innovation-has-always-delivered-more-long-run-employment-not-less (accessed Mar. 27, 2014).

CHAPTER 2

Disruption as a Way of Life

Talk of psychohistory and precrime might seem better suited to a science fiction convention than an executive briefing. However, the more our world changes, the more we need to question our assumptions. And, therein lies the trap—we've become so accustomed to change that we don't even realize that it's happening any more.

There's an apocryphal parable about a frog in boiling water. While not true, it suggests that a frog's nervous system is sufficiently under-developed and that when it's put in cold water and the water is slowly heated, the frog won't know it's in danger until it's boiled alive. Apart from being pretty cruel to the frog, it carries another message. We, collectively, are that frog.

Our world has changed. It's changing at such an accelerating rate that we've lost track of the speed. Perception is relative; at walking speed, someone running past us seems swift. On a highway, someone overtaking us seems fairly lethargic. To the runner, though, the two cars are terrifyingly fast.

Alvin Toffler, one of the world's most famous futurologists, coined the term "future shock" in 1970.[1] In his book *Future Shock* he argued that too much change in too short a period of time would lead to shattering stress and disorientation. This would create a society characterized by social paralysis and personal disconnection. The rate of change he predicted has come to pass. However, he got the impact backward.

We, as a society, have looked change in the face and laughed. What's fantastical one year is commonplace the next. In some cases, even within months; how many times in the last year have you found a device or application you couldn't live without only to have it become such a central part of your life that you don't even realize it's there anymore?

There's danger in this complacency. Just because we're used to the water getting warmer, it doesn't mean that we're out of danger. The rest of this chapter will review five key trends that will fundamentally change the way we view the world over the next decade. These are:

1. The Age of Uncertainty
2. The Emergence of Big Data
3. The Rise of the Rōnin
4. The Knowledge Rush
5. Systematized Chaos

Again, this isn't futurism; they are all already happening. Thus far, their impacts are still relatively small. With advance knowledge, a competent leader still has time to take advantage of them.

THE AGE OF UNCERTAINTY

Change will continue to accelerate and the resulting social complexity and economic interconnectedness will increase the frequency of unintended consequences and unexpected events. Dynamic management focused on emphasizing robustness rather than pure efficiency will become common. Leaders will need to become comfortable with uncertainty, planning for "unknown unknowns," and trust sophisticated monitoring engines that leverage big data.

Ours is a magical time. Every day, we do things that would have been in realms of science fiction not even three decades ago. Twenty years ago, an international telephone call from New York to London cost approximately a dollar a minute.[2] Today, we can videoconference for free on a device that fits in our pocket. The iPhone 5s, a high-specification mobile phone released in 2013, is faster than the MacBook Pro released in 2008, a high-end laptop. In less than five years, we've created a device that's smaller, faster, has greater fidelity, offers mobile connectivity, and has over double the battery life.[3]

Over 23 years ago, *Star Trek* fantasized about the Personal Access Display Device, a hand-held computer with a touch-screen interface. In 2010, Apple launched the iPad, making *Star Trek*'s PADDs real and affordable. In isolation, that's mind-blowing. However, the most fascinating thing about them is that in less than three years from when they were launched, the tablet as a personal computing device was taken for granted and largely commonplace.

The examples are endless. Toys can be shipped and delivered almost overnight from China that quite literally have millions of times more processing power than Apollo 11. Three-dimensional printers are commercially available and consumer friendly. Not only are electric cars such as the Tesla commercially available but Google is road-testing driverless cars. Facebook and Sony are developing commercially viable virtual reality systems. While we're still waiting for our flying cars, the world's closer to the future than ever before.

Communication and information is instantaneous, pervasive, and always-on; no matter where we are, we're plugged in. To a kid, the idea of being involuntarily unplugged is almost inconceivable. With fourth-generation mobile connectivity and portable solar rechargers, even camping no longer offers an escape! The scale of this change is subtle; it sneaks up on you. Given enough exposure, even magic becomes mundane. Therein lies the danger.

The world is changing around us at an accelerating rate. As it does so, it changes us, for good or bad. Much like the industrial revolution, it's not clear yet how this technology will impact society. Thus far, we know that it offers social and professional advantages to those who have it and know how to use it. And, quantitative analysis has shown that access and use of information technology is dependent on income and access to education.[4] This carries with it a stark implication: access (or lack thereof) to information runs the risk of creating an entire social strata of "haves" and "have-nots."

We live in a world where social, cultural and economic capital is dependent on one's ability to connect, communicate, and create through technology. In this world, lacking these skills can create a true digital divide, one that has intergenerational implications. As change accelerates, it becomes that much harder for the disadvantaged to keep up.

While this is clearly a global concern, its implications also fall closer to home. The 2011 U.S. Census showed that only 71.7 percent of households accessed the Internet. While not terribly concerning in isolation, what *is* concerning is the lowest usage rates clustered around the less educated and those with low incomes.[5] It's a measure of the role that technology plays in our lives that some argue that this digital divide is a threat not only to economic mobility and social stability but even democratic representation.[6]

At the micro-level, information is power, both for the individual and the collective. It gives us the ability to network and connect with lost friends. However, it's more than that. The ability to connect and communicate has already supported revolutions in Egypt, Tunisia, and Libya.[7] What affects the individual has also had an effect on the organization. Globalization is easier than it's ever been and location is rarely a barrier to business. At the macro-level, that same decline in communication costs has affected global trading patterns and competitive price advantage, especially in the case of differentiated products.[8]

Digitization has and is fueling disruption. Despite this, the fundamentals of business have not changed. Success still requires innovation, differentiation, and a relentless focus on efficient execution. What *has* changed is the dynamic that information plays in this mix. While information has always conferred advantage, the sheer volume of information available has changed its relative contribution to success.

The greatest irony of our age is that despite having access to more information than ever before, we remain more in the dark than ever. It's true that we generate tremendous amounts of data. In any given day, the digital footprint we leave dwarfs the data we have of entire civilizations. We know more about what the world bought for lunch yesterday than we do about the entirety of ancient Egypt.

It's also true that rather than making it easier to understand our world, all this information instead makes it more confusing. Connectivity comes with a price; the more tightly coupled our industries and lives become, the harder it becomes to predict unintentional outcomes. What could once be said around the watercooler with relative impunity carries different implications when said on Facebook or Twitter. Complexity and interconnectedness bring with them uncertainty, both personally and professionally.

The financial crisis of 2007 was a poignant example of how severe this uncertainty has become. The market at the time was characterized by easy credit. It also saw significant growth of subprime loans from under 10 percent of the total mortgage market to over 20 percent at their peak. The use of complex financial instruments such as mortgage-backed securities, credit default swaps, and synthetic collateralized debt obligations (CDOs) was commonplace.

Together, these established a highly complex financial system that not only increased the distance between the physical asset and the final purchaser but also multiplied the number of actors involved with any particular product. While this theoretically offered the advantage of diversification through blended assets, it also reduced overall transparency and risk lineage. It got to the point where the products became so complicated that some, George Soros included, felt that the authorities and regulators could no longer calculate the risk and instead were forced to simply "take the word" of the banks issuing the products.[9] Eventually, the catastrophe happened; the outcomes of the liquidity crisis are well-known, and in many countries, are still being felt.

The unexpected twist in the story was the level of uncertainty around who would be affected by the progressive fallout and, if so, how badly they would be affected. Our financial markets had become so interconnected and tightly coupled that by the time of the Great Recession, banks in far corners of the world had unknowingly acquired overleveraged or even negative-value U.S. assets. Unpicking this Gordian knot and accurately determining true exposures was difficult and, in some cases, arguably impossible. Systemic risk, financial innovation, regulatory evasion, and complexity may have caused the crisis. Uncertainty, however, characterized the aftermath.

Despite all our scientific, technical, and intellectual advancements, this will be the defining characteristic of our time. We've entered the *era of uncertainty*, a post–information age period of sustained disruption and change. The digital revolution is no longer a revolution; it's simply the new normal. We spend large amounts of time trying to manage our "known knowns" and "known unknowns." Unfortunately, in a world where economic, social, and professional connections are growing exponentially, so do the opportunities for "unknown unknowns."

Incumbents find it increasingly difficult to predict who their next big competitor will be. Facebook came from nowhere and disrupted MySpace in less than two years. BlackBerry and Nokia went from being market leaders to shadows of their former selves, not by the hand of another telecommunications company but by an almost-failed computer company (Apple) and a search company (Google). Financial institutions find themselves under threat not only from hackers and organized crime in specific countries but from disenfranchised teenagers and young adults wearing Guy Fawkes masks.

Systemic complexity creates uncertainty. Nassim Taleb, author and statistician, talks of Black Swans, highly improbably events that have an extreme impact should they occur.[10] By definition, these are outliers and the odds of any of these individually happening remains low. However, the *frequency* with which we experience these events through the age of uncertainty will increase as our world becomes more complex.

Every action has the potential for intentional and unintentional consequences. As we scale our interactions, so do we scale our potential for Black Swans. Most dangerously of all, adapting to this accelerating rate of change requires us to acknowledge that which we know is dwarfed by that which we don't. This isn't the first time we've gone through such a massive shift. However, history has shown that times of rapid disruption usually lead to drastically changed social and economic structures.

Rather than planning for the known, the era of uncertainty will require organizations and individuals to manage and live based on adaptability, flexibility, and robustness. In an environment characterized by rapid and volatile change, the concept of a static business model will eventually seem as archaic and quaint as the horse and wagon.

THE EMERGENCE OF BIG DATA

> The information contained in big data will reduce experience-based barriers to entry in many industry sectors. The traditional separation between many industry verticals will start to collapse and for these industries, differentiation purely based on experience and sector knowledge will progressively evaporate. Leaders will need to become comfortable with the constant threat of disruption from nontraditional competitors.

The sudden focus on big data is more than just a technical fad. It's a manifestation of a broader zeitgeist.

"Big data" has become one of the most used and overused catchphrases. It's getting to the point where if something doesn't have the term somewhere in the brief, someone's not doing their job. Just because it's popular, however, doesn't mean it's overstated. We've been through the information revolution. We've seen knowledge workers come and go. We've even got our head around Web 2.0 as we rocket through Web 3.0 on our way to Web 4.0.

Big data dwarfs all of these, not only for the decade but for the rest of our natural lives as well. Rather than just being hype, our sheer volume of discussion reflects the impact people suspect it will have. It's an idea whose time has come.

Ideas are fascinating. They don't exist in any real sense; they're a shared delusion, carrying us beyond our physicality. Abstraction is powerful and in some ways, it's what distinguishes us as a species. Jean Piaget, acclaimed developmental psychologist, theorized that it's only in our final stage of cognitive development, the formal operational stage, that we make the transition from concrete thinking to abstract logic.[11]

As babies, we are phenomenists. We define our world based on our personal experience, not on the physicality of the objects around us. When we hide behind a sheet, it's arguable that from the baby's perspective, we're not just hiding. We've literally temporarily ceased to exist. As we develop, we progressively make the leap from naturalist interpretation of physical objects to symbolic representation, abstract thought, and metacognition.

The significance of this step is enormous and yet it's often overlooked. While nowhere near a primary measure of self-worth or community value, some have suggested that as many as two-thirds of adults never reach the formal operational stage.[12] We refer to the "economy" or "market" and yet, what is it? To a child, it's a physical place where one can go to buy carrots. It's down the street and to the left, somewhere that smells of earth and spices.

In the abstract, it's a synthetic aggregation of all possible markets in all possible spaces at any point in time. In a multidimensional sense, it's a superposition of everything we can't measure or observe, all at once. It includes even stranger things like derivatives, collateralized debt obligations, and currency created through fractional reserve banking. These exist not even as numbers on a piece of paper but as magnetic fields on hard drives scattered across the globe.

Despite being unreal in a very literal sense, they have the power to change our world. Ideas aren't real. And yet, they replicate, mutate, and at some stage, terminate. They hold a mirror up to our cultural gestalt, reflecting that which is most important to us at a point in time. Richard Dawkins, author and evolutionary biologist, coined the term *meme* to describe this almost evolutionary process of cultural transmission.[13] Successful memes replicate and mutate. Unsuccessful memes stagnate and eventually die. Thanks to the Internet, popular and culturally relevant concepts propagate at the speed of light, ignoring national and social barriers. Resonant concepts grow in strength while irrelevant concepts decline. One only needs to look at doge—so impressive; much sharing.[14]

Memes survive through cultural relevance. And, not all do. Our linguistic landscape is scattered with "lost words," terms that for some reason fell out of favor. The archaic term, *California widow*, seems strange without the background context of a gold rush. *Tyromancy*, the process of divining by the coagulation of cheese, is not as common as it once was. Our language, culture, and ideas represent a snapshot of what we care about and are interested in.

Big data *is* one of these concepts. We talk about it because it's here and it's affecting us. Like most big ideas, though, it's not just what it means now. It's also what it means for our future. But first, what *is* "big data"?

It's more than just lots of data. Most people have heard of Moore's law,[15] the trend for the number of transistors on a microprocessor to double roughly every 18 months. In less technical terms, computers tend to double in speed about every two years. It's one of the reasons why the iPhone 5s (released in late 2013) slightly beats the original MacBook Air (released in early 2008) in processing benchmarks.

Fewer people have heard of Kryder's law, the trend for storage density to outstrip processing capacity improvements.[16] Our ability to store information has been consistently growing at a rate faster than a chip's ability to process information.

We're generating more data than ever before. We've been through the *structured era*, where we've needed to capture billing information, personal information, financial information, and transaction information.* Without an address, there's nowhere to send a bill. Without a name, there's no-one to address a bill to. Without an account or a credit card, there's no way of processing payment. And without a transaction, there's no way of knowing how much to bill.

Capturing, integrating, and exposing this information was hard enough. Organizations have spent hundreds of millions of dollars building warehouses and developing strategies simply to cope with this data. But, we've managed.

As daunting as this was, we're now deep in the middle of the *social era*. While structured data is useful for computers, we prefer text and pictures, often called *unstructured* data. It's estimated that every year, the average worker writes about a book's worth of email.[17] By that measure, any given office is producing as much content as a small-scale publisher, event taking into account the time people spend talking on Twitter, blogging, or catching up on Facebook.

We're not only generating more data than ever before, we're creating *new types* of data. Every photo has within it people, places, and even events. Every status update has mood, location, and often intent. Not only are we having to deal with format changes from structured to

---

*Structured data in its simplest sense is data that can be organized in a predefined manner. For example, telephone numbers follow a fixed structure as do postcodes. The primary advantage of structured data is ease of analysis. When one knows what the data will always look like, it's relatively easy to analyze. The primary disadvantage is the constraints it implies. Anything that doesn't fit into the predefined structure must be discarded.

unstructured data; we're having to deal with how best to extract latent information from raw data.

However, this pales in comparison to the next wave. e-Commerce gave us visibility over how we spend and save our money. Social gave us visibility over what we're interested in, what we're doing, and who we know. However, there's more. Increasingly, it's no longer about what *we're* choosing to say or do. Our devices are doing it for us.

We're just at the start of the *sensor era*. Smart devices are "chatty." They're smart *because* they have the ability to be chatty. Sensor data has always been around; it's just that historically it hasn't been terribly interesting outside of systems monitoring and maintenance. OBD-II, a real-time onboard diagnostics bus, was made mandatory for all cars sold in the United States as far back as 1996. Intended to support emissions testing, the protocol also gave real-time access to an exhaustive set of statistics on (among other things) vehicle speed, accelerator positions, fuel type being used, and vehicle identification numbers.

This data served an important purpose; detailed data made preventative maintenance easier. Given the right programming, embedded systems can give advance warning of their potential failure. Rather than being the exception, the model used by OBD-II has become the norm. Anyone who's saved their data from a failing hard drive probably has the S.M.A.R.T. (Self-Monitoring, Analysis, and Reporting Technology) monitoring system to thank for it. In making our devices smarter, rather than reducing the data our devices are generating, we've *increased* it. The Boeing 787 Dreamliner, a prime example of modern aviation engineering, generates approximately half a terabyte of sensor data *every flight*.[18]

Lest one think that this is exclusively the domain of transportation or heavy machinery, our personal devices are doing exactly the same thing. The iPhone 5s launched with the energy-efficient M7 chip, a device specifically designed to track motion and movement. Pair that with a GPS and a global database that geolocates wireless networks and any given phone can easily capture and track the most minute of our movements throughout the day.

Every time we make a call, the communication network needs to know where we are, whom we're calling, and how long we spoke to them. Without that metadata, it's impossible to close the circuit and have a conversation. Smart meters track electricity use on a near-real-time basis, giving energy companies direct visibility over intraday energy consumption patterns. Relative to historical standards, the sheer volume of this data is staggering. A typical telecommunications carrier will generate a few terabytes of call detail data every month. A typical energy company that has access to smart meters now has access to more data in a single day than it has had over the last hundred years.

This, fundamentally, is the challenge and opportunity of big data. We're generating *more* data than ever before. We're generating more *types* of data than ever before. And, we're generating it *faster* than ever before. Big data represents an inflection point in what we consider "normal" relative to historical volumes, variety, and velocity of data.*

The challenges that go with this are obvious. To be useful, all this data needs to be stored, accessed, interrogated, analyzed, and used. Unfortunately, the "new normal" of big data gels poorly with how most organizations have made their technology investments. Platforms designed for terabytes of data rarely work well when asked to scale to petabytes or even exabytes. Ask a mechanic to reverse-engineer the family station-wagon into a Formula-1 car and see what happens.

The opportunities are a bit more subtle. It's easy to argue that big data is just the latest version of "data." Simplistically, this is true. However, it's more than this. At the turn of the century, when society looks back and takes stock, the emergence of the term will coincide with the turning point at which the nature of industry, government, and society started to change. As did those who lived through the industrial revolution or heard Gutenberg first speak of his miraculous machine, we have only started to feel the disruption big data will bring with it.

That's a big statement, but it's a valid one. Information asymmetries are well known in economics.[19] In an ideal world, every transaction involves a perfect match between desire and need. Prices are perfect, transactions are frictionless, and barriers to entry are almost nonexistent. However, efficient markets require perfect information, an unrealistic ideal. Where some know more than others, the market operates imperfectly, sometimes outright failing. Prices become distorted and significant barriers to entry emerge, typically controlled by the incumbents who have the advantage of better knowledge.

---

*The 3 *V*s of Big Data were originally coined by Doug Laney as early as 2001 in his report, "3D Data Management: Controlling Data Volume, Velocity, and Variety." For more information, see http://blogs.gartner.com/doug-laney/files/2012/01/ad949-3D-Data-Management-Controlling-Data-Volume-Velocity-and-Variety.pdf.

Perfect information is a fantasy. But, what happens when the fantasy keeps getting closer to reality?

If every single action we make can be captured and shared, where does imperfect information then sit? Our understanding of economics changes fundamentally, as does our understanding of what society looks like. What does privacy mean in a world where every personal and professional relationship is captured as a matter of course? What does energy conservation policy look like where it's possible to understand not only how every single person around the world is consuming electricity in real-time but what the immediate measurable effects of policy changes are? What does drug development look like where you not only have access to the entire world's gene profile but can monitor unknown side effects and unintentional but potentially lethal drug cocktails, not through hypothetical testing but through continuous population monitoring?

The true potential of big data is not better customer engagement. It's not better economic management. It's not even better public safety. These are all byproducts, mere side-effects of information efficiency. What big data implies is a different world, one where many aspects of society and the broader economy become characterized by the potential of near-perfect information, one that is fundamentally disrupted, regardless of industry sector.

These are lofty statements, hyperbolic even. What they are not, however, is unprecedented. The invention of the combustion engine during the industrial revolution disrupted industries, economies, social structures, and even our definition of time.[20] The sudden shift of capital and political influence toward the Vanderbilts, the Rockefellers, and the Carnegies wasn't a coincidence of history; it was a clear demonstration of how disruptive events and technologies change the world as we know it.

Information has always equated to power. Entire sectors have been built on this power inequality, whether it's at the micro-level of selling used goods through to the macro-level of financial markets. Knowing how the market operates and what signals to rely on has been a strong barrier to entry for centuries. In the absence of quantitative information, one has to rely on experience, and without experience, one is powerless.

Big data cracks this edifice; when data becomes plentiful and accessible, the need for experience declines. There's still an argument for monopoly in this—own the data, own the market. Unfortunately, there's almost always a back door. Whether it's through investment, acquisition, collection, or partnering, most data is up for grabs in some form. And, with this data comes the ability to understand the market as well as or better than the incumbents.

This isn't an abstract fantasy. This is already happening. Supermarkets like the Australian brand Coles are getting banking licenses and presenting real competition to the traditional Australian banks, protected as they are by the four pillars policy. The same is true for telecommunications companies such as Rogers in Canada. Nonbanking institutions like PayPal are inserting themselves into the payment chain and actively dis-intermediating the banks. Media streamers like Netflix and Amazon are generating their own content and diverting subscribers away from cable providers.

If all you have is experience, it's only a matter of time until someone smarter than you works out how to use the data to disrupt you. Big data is more than just more information; it represents the beginning of the end of industry experience as a core competitive advantage. If your differentiation is based purely on sector knowledge, replication is simply a case of getting access to enough data to come to similar conclusions. Thirty years of experience counts for nothing if a graduate can develop an algorithm that comes to the same conclusion as an expert.

RISE OF THE RŌNIN

A structural tightening of the labor market for skilled professionals will increase the competitive advantage offered by human capital. Salaries will rise and signals that indicate competency will become increasingly inaccurate. Leaders will need to become experts in human capital identification, development, and retention, not just experts in their preferred areas of competency.

Our future is one of uncertainty caused by disruption. However, in disruption there is opportunity. Big data may be the key to unlocking this opportunity, but without an operator, every key is useless.

Business analytics is the catalyst that unlocks value from data.[21] Some have even gone so far as to say it may become a dominant force of competitive differentiation.[22] It is, however a complex discipline. It requires a mélange of skills including mathematics, pragmatism, change management, project management, software development, systems architecture, data management, programming, and business knowledge. Given this highly unrealistic capability set, it shouldn't come as any surprise that skilled practitioners are in high demand. What may come as a surprise is how *significant* the demand is for these people.

A survey of forum members conducted in 2013 by KDNuggets, a data-mining community, found that average salaries had increased by 13 percent between 2012 and 2013 in the United States and Canada and 12 percent globally.[23] Lest one think this was a one-off data point, a similar survey conducted in the United Kingdom by Harnham, a recruiter, found that 55 percent of respondents saw their salary increase at double the rate of inflation between 2012 and 2013.[24] The Institute of Analytics Professionals of Australia, a professional association for analytics practitioners, found similar results. In their 2013 annual skills and salary survey, over 70 percent of respondents had seen their salaries increase moderately or significantly in the three years prior.[25]

This isn't a cyclical shift. This increase in demand represents a structural shift in the labor market driven by a fundamental change in the nature of business. With data comes the opportunity to do things better, and doing so requires people.

To monetize their data, organizations need access to people with the right skills, mindset, and experience. This isn't easy. Relatively speaking, technology is fairly straightforward. Human capital, however, is hard. While structural shifts like this are not totally unprecedented, the speed at which this transformation is happening is somewhat staggering. Gartner estimated in late 2012 that by 2015, the rise of big data would create over 4 million IT jobs globally, of which 1.9 million would be in the United States. This number grows even larger when second- and third-order effects are taken into account. If each big data–related role creates another three downstream roles, the need to analyze and leverage big data will create demand for another 6 million jobs in the United States.[26]

This speed of transition is creating ripples in the labor market. Of these potential jobs, Gartner estimates that only a third will end up being filled. Again, lest one think that this is an anomaly, McKinsey, a consultancy, came to similar conclusions.[27] Looking further into the future, by 2018 McKinsey estimates that the United States alone would experience a shortfall of as many as 190,000 skilled data scientists and over 1.5 million managers and analysts capable of taking advantage of these insights. In percentage terms, this represents a 50 to 60 percent gap between supply and demand.

Estimates of the shortfall vary between analysts. What's consistent, however, is the trend toward a significant labor market imbalance. The root cause behind this imbalance is not education. Were it so, the rapid rise in skilled postgraduates from China and India might offer a solution. Sadly, as will be covered in Chapter 7, getting the most out of big data requires experience, business knowledge, as well as technical capabilities. These develop best through practical experience.

In his book *Outliers*, Gladwell suggested that it takes approximately 10,000 hours to become the best in any particular domain.[28] This is especially true in business analytics where cross-functional coordination and experience is the norm rather than the exception. Even the best postgraduate is only operating at half-potential without this critical experience.

Some of the impacts of this imbalance are obvious. Salaries will continue to increase, especially for those who meet the profile of value creators rather than statisticians or pure analysts. The limiting factor for many organizations will become their ability to *find* and *keep* the right people, regardless of how well funded projects are. And, labor mobility for those with the right skills will remain high with the most skilled people crossing roles, industries, and even borders to wherever the offering's the most attractive.

The *age of uncertainty* will correspond with the *rise of the rōnin*, a new class of worker that is highly mobile, highly skilled, and yet motivated by factors more complex than money alone. Most are familiar with the samurai, the middle and upper echelons of the warrior class in feudal Japan. Following a complex set of rules known as *bushidō*, the samurai attempted to embody a moral code grounded in loyalty, frugality, and honor. Comparatively well-educated in Japanese society, they swore fealty to a single master. Moral transgressions carried severe penalties; for a truly disgraced samurai, the only option was seppuku, a ritualized form of suicide.

While many know of the samurai, fewer know of the rōnin. On losing their master, not all samurai decided to strictly follow bushidō. Whether it was through desertion or death, some disgraced samurai would become mobile and seek alternative employment. Still carrying their dual swords, they walked a fine line. Those who sought regular, respectable work became mercenaries or enforcers, defending caravans and being bodyguards. Those who sought more opportunistic employment often gravitated toward the gangs, becoming petty criminals or bandits. Their relative lack of responsibilities compared to their loyal brethren often led to a more festive reputation, doing whatever they wanted without any respect to their "betters."

To be a rōnin was to be forced to reinvent oneself, a not insignificant challenge under the Tokugawa shogunate. Equally though, during the Edo period's constrained social order and formalized classist society, the rōnin experienced a level of social mobility and freedom that was unavailable to most, even if that freedom came at a price. Educated, skilled, and experienced, their abilities opened doors that remained closed to many. The lack of predefined direction forced the rōnin to chase that which they were most comfortable or interested in. For some, it was simply survival. For many, it was profit. For others, it was the opportunity to regain honor.

Disruption may not have created the rōnin. It did, however, help them grow. Economic growth, forced land confiscation and concentration under the 300 regional Daiymo, and regulatory change saw the rōnin grow substantially during the Edo period. While the current disruption has different causes, we are seeing the creation of a new class of worker, one that is highly skilled, in significant global demand, and yet motivated by factors far more complex than money alone. These modern-day rōnin are equally as mobile as their namesakes. Thanks to a continually tightening labor market, they have unparalleled professional mobility. Rather than being constrained by industry sector, their skills are highly portable between industries.

While not as experienced or effective as a pure specialist, their ability to use mathematical or computational methods to solve complex problems breaks down many of the barriers between industry sectors. Their raw mathematical talent opens doors and opportunities unavailable to most. Inevitably, their skills lead to significant salaries.

According to the Institute of Analytics Professionals, the median salary of a person employed in the field in Australia is over twice the national median salary!

For these individuals, money is always a consideration. Being largely scientific and numerical in mindset, they usually well understand the opportunity cost of staying in a comparatively low-paid position. However, the leverage they carry creates an interesting dynamic. Maslow's hierarchy of needs provides an excellent lens through which their thinking patterns can be explained.[29] They have no true fear of unemployment; a rising tide lifts all boats. Even in a recessionary market, the demand for their skills continues to rise. With their physiological and safety needs easily catered for, they look for more.

For many, being part of a strong team with a good fit becomes a major consideration. Belonging, therefore, becomes more than an afterthought; if they don't enjoy working with their managers and peers, they can usually easily enough find another team to be a part of. Whether it's through forming personal bonds or being exposed to new ideas, social anxiety or being understimulated/underchallenged can easily be a trigger to look for something else. Without a strong cultural fit, any role they take will inevitably be a transitory one.

Beyond this, many look for esteem and achievement. Sometimes, this takes the form of internal and external recognition and reputation. Other times, it takes the form of applying their skills to solve real problems. These types of people look for more than a nine-to-five job; they want their skills to have an impact on something. Without a sense of personal growth or achievement, they will look elsewhere. Others seek self-actualization. They look to advance knowledge, solve social ills, or otherwise demonstrate mastery of their skills on a daily basis.

Like the rōnin of old, their existence will create both challenge and opportunity. Without them, many organizations will be unable to compete. They will see their data assets go to waste as their competitors take leaps ahead. Like these modern-day rōnin or loathe them, they will become a critical part of every operation.

Most will be comparatively expensive but largely substitutable; a warrior is a warrior. However, some will be truly transformative, blending analytical, domain, and value-creating abilities into an enabler for competitive advantage. Ranging from maladjusted prima donnas to transformative visionaries, the leverage they will carry will create no end of headaches. The power they bring will be enviable, as long as it can be effectively channeled.

THE KNOWLEDGE RUSH

> In a digital world, absolute control of unique information assets is a source of competitive differentiation. Leaders will need to be aware that by missing out on capturing, acquiring, or augmenting unique sources, they may well be unwittingly permanently locking themselves out of developing markets.

The *age of uncertainty* will lead to new opportunities, many of them centered around the use of *big data* and reliant on *the rise of the rōnin*. These new assets carry with them significant implications.

Few things have the ability to redistribute power or wealth as significantly as the discovery of a new class of asset. The impact can be highly variable. Sometimes, it can lead to the creation of a new empire. Other times, it can lead to improved income mobility and personal independence. One thing, however, is constant—in times of economic disruption, whoever controls the asset controls the future.

The degree to which this can change the world shouldn't be underestimated. In June 1870, John D. Rockefeller founded Standard Oil as his entry-point into the rapidly growing oil market. The earliest records on file show 1,200 barrels being skimmed from Pennsylvania in 1858. Only 12 years later, when Standard Oil was launched, Pennsylvania was producing an estimated 5.2 million barrels.[30] By the end of the 1870s, Standard Oil was in control of over 90 percent of oil refinery in the United States.[31] To put this in perspective, Pennsylvania alone in 1880 was producing 26 million barrels with the price per barrel having roughly doubled since 1861.[32]

Controlling this new asset was highly profitable; it helped build Rockefeller's empire and contributed significantly to making him arguably the wealthiest man in American history. It's estimated that in today's (inflation-adjusted) dollars, Rockefeller would have been worth almost US$1.5 billion, 1/65 of total U.S. GDP at the time.[33]

Vanderbilt, another magnate, followed a similar model through progressively controlling the railroads.

Controlling a unique asset confers power. The ongoing digitization of our world is subtly yet surely seeding the latest disruption; big data is the new oil. Everything we do leaves a data footprint and the future will be like today, only more so. Every time our kids play a game on their latest console, they'll be watched. Whom they play with, how long they play, what they do, even how quickly they play through their games will be registered. Every time we watch cable, our viewing patterns will be captured. People will analyze how many times we've changed the channel, what shows we've watched, even whether we've muted the TV during particular advertisements. Every time we leave the house, our telephone providers will be monitoring where we go, whom we communicate with, and even what information we're looking up while we're mobile.

To most, this might sound like a rather dystopian future. However, it's already here.

Microsoft and Sony both included various online infrastructure as part of their game console offerings in 2006. Through tracking activity, interaction, and effectiveness of play, these platforms allowed players to connect with other players and receive achievements or trophies for finishing particular tasks in games. By necessity, their actions and friends had to be centrally tracked and managed, complete with time-stamps for historical purposes.

Termed "in-game telemetry," this data proved tremendously valuable in understanding how players interact with their games and other people. It gave developers the ability to see where gamers are and aren't succeeding within the game. It gave marketers the ability to see which aspects of the game gamers are most interested in. And, it gave publishers the ability to make objective decisions about where they should be investing. This is a bigger deal than one might initially suppose.

Grand Theft Auto V, a part of a well-known gaming franchise, was estimated to cost over $250 million to develop and market.[34] The sheer scale of investment in games surprises many. What's even more surprising, however, is that most players never even *see* everything they paid for. A common industry rule of thumb is that less than 10 percent of players will ever play through to the end of a game.[35]

Cutting back the total investment is a no-brainer. The problem is in working out what to cut. It's true that every gamer may only experience a small proportion of the total game content in a free-roaming game. Unfortunately, because they have the freedom to explore, the content *they* see will often be different from the content *other* gamers see. Given that every second of content costs money to design, code, create the assets, and bug-test, being able to see what gamers are and aren't interested in offers significant insight into where investments *should* occur.

In a talk given at GDC 2010, a game development conference, BioWare (a developer owned by Electronic Arts) outlined the sophistication this analysis can go to.[36] *Dragon Age: Origins* was a large game. With over 800,000 lines of dialog, more than 180 areas to explore, greater than 300,000 lines of scripted code, 18 different character design options, and more than 300 abilities, the game was simply too large to exhaustively test and analyze. Rather than guess, they decided to track player usage patterns during the development cycle, using those insights to better inform game design.

To aid design, they tracked over 1.1 million play sessions across 1,141 machines, generating over 250GB of data across approximately 38 million data points. When analyzed, this helped them to identify movement patterns, boring points, and even pacing issues, helping them to design a game that was eventually a critical success.

This isn't a one-off example; similar techniques are used at organizations such as Bungie (the creator of *Halo*, another blockbuster franchise), Microsoft, and Sony.[37] The value of this data is immeasurable; in some cases, it can make the difference between a game that makes a profit and a game that bankrupts the company.

A similar story is playing out elsewhere. LG was embroiled in a PR disaster in late 2013 when it emerged that regardless of consumer preferences their smart TVs would upload viewing patterns back to LG for analysis within their "LG Smart Ad" offering.[38] Designed to enable more relevant advertising, this data included what channels people watched, the name of the channel, and even the names of any media files watched. The public backlash to this involuntary data sharing was understandable.

Regardless of industry, having access to low-level behavioral data is invaluable. By necessity, telecommunications carriers need to be able to triangulate and communicate with every phone on their network. Without this information, they can't get a signal to the phone. This meta-data can be similarly captured and stored, along with whom one communicates with and for how long. It can be used to identify influence, understand preferences, and allow real-time location-based advertising. Relevancy becomes more than just the right product at the right time; it extends to include the right place and even the right mindset.

Access to this information can make or break companies. Being denied access to data can shift the balance of power between partners so significantly that failure can become a very real threat. In the high-risk market of game development, a single failed game can be enough to bankrupt a studio. Control access to data and the barriers to entry can become insurmountable. Gain access to data and barriers to entry may even evaporate.

There's a hidden battle taking place right now, one that involves aspirational magnates jockeying for position. Exclusive control over unique data can generate differentiation in its own right. They're even enough to break otherwise strong partnerships.

Much was made about Apple's poor-performing Apple Maps application when it launched. Previously, Apple had included Google's Map product as a bundled application, broadly perceived by the market as the better application. Despite this, Apple decided to part ways with Google when it launched iOS6, setting its own application as standard and forcing Google to resubmit its application through the Apple App store.

The decision had repercussions. Apple weathered a great deal of negative publicity over the change, largely due to the poor-quality data within its internally developed application. One of the most glaring omissions was the lack of a Statue of Liberty on Liberty Island! Given that Apple *must* have known that there would backlash, why would the company do it?

The decision to part ways was made for many reasons, Google's interest in having more branding visibility within the app being a particular sticking point, according to insiders. However, it was more than that. Without access to high-quality geospatial data, it's impossible to even think about offering geographically targeted services to customers or suppliers. Being locked out of such a significant channel becomes a real threat to customer engagement. And, the only way to gain entry is to source and improve the data somehow.

Even though they still had a year left on their contract with Google, Apple recognized that it had no choice in the battle between the two titans. Mapping is hard. It requires tremendous amounts of accurate data, continually updated. And, Google had a head start. In 2004, the company acquired ZipDash, Where2, and Keyhole Inc., all companies focused on geospatial data collection, analysis, and distribution. In 2006, Google acquired Endoxon; in 2007, ImageAmerica; in 2010, Quiksee. Google "got" the need for data early in the picture and Apple was caught out.

The only answer was to take the punch. Apple's lack of foresight cost them a great deal of customer loyalty. The damage was so great that Tim Cook, the CEO, ended up publicly apologizing for the lack of quality in their homegrown application. Building equivalent data takes years and Apple was caught on the back foot.

Even today, the battle continues. As of mid-2013, Google had just acquired Waze for US$1.1 billion, an Israeli mapping company focused on crowd-sourced traffic analysis based on social data. This was Google's single largest acquisition after Motorola, DoubleClick, and YouTube. Google's latest acquisition of Nest in early 2014 for $3 billion is seen as a gambit by many to start collecting data from *inside* our homes, using smoke alarms and thermostats to understand how we live and behave when we're alone.

On their side, Apple quickly acquired Locationary, a crowd-sourced local data company, and HopStop, a city-navigation app. In late 2013, Apple also acquired Embark and Broadmap for undisclosed sums. Without the ability to generate, analyze, and deliver geospatial information to their customers, each would be left with a significant chink in their armor. In this arms race, the best weapon is data.

Like a gold rush, this *knowledge rush* is seeing organizations try to get a head start over their competitors by buying exclusive access to data. Like spice, gold, or oil, information is the latest disruptive asset. Given enough effort, technology can be replicated. Data, however, cannot—it requires a rich set of historical activity and behaviors. By gaining exclusive rights to data, either through express ownership or negotiated licensing arrangements, organizations can lock out their competitors, sometimes indefinitely. These titans move globally, setting up sites and acquiring data in the same way Standard Oil once gained horizontal and vertical control over their industry segment. Information is power and influence, and those who don't move quickly will rapidly find that they have neither.

SYSTEMATIZED CHAOS

> The emergence of increasingly complex systems will create management structures and operational systems that are inherently brittle and prone to failure. Leaders will need to become comfortable with managing systems that are inherently unmanageable through the use of crowdsourcing, back-ended operational analytics, and complex adaptive systems.

One of the biggest drivers behind *the age of uncertainty* is complexity. Simple rules can lead to surprisingly complex systems. Somewhat counterintuitively, they can also sometimes be the solution.

Consider, for example, an insect. Individually, an ant has a brain smaller than the head of a pin. This size comes with a significant cost: processing power. On average, an ant has approximately 250,000 neurons, a rather unimpressive statistic. The average honey bee is an intellectual giant in comparison with approximately a million neurons.[39] For comparison, a typical human has between 19 and 23 billion neurons.[40]

Despite having .001 percent of the cognitive processing power of a human, ants don't get an easy ride. They lead a challenging life. They need to forage. They need to communicate with the colony. They need to feed themselves as well as the queen. And, they need to survive. Nature is cruel; there are no freebies for the weak.

Adversity, however, breeds innovation—in the face of overwhelming challenges, life finds a way. What the individual can't overcome, the collective can sometimes solve. Ants, bees, and other hive-based creatures have evolved a tremendously innovative and efficient solution: crowdsourcing.[41] Energy isn't cheap for a creature as small as an ant. Brainpower is costly. However, reproduction *is* cheap; while it's expensive to develop a brain and survive, it's cheap to replicate. Rather than try to develop the intelligence to handle complex solutions, in some situations it's more efficient to act locally and rely on the wisdom of crowds.

From an ant's perspective, the world is infinite. In the three to six months most ants live, an ant running full speed all day every day might potentially cover over 600 kilometers. Allowing time to rest, breed, and eat, seeing the world would take hundreds of generations. Memory and intelligence, in that context, is worth little; when life is short, passing on one's experience does little to help the next generation.

And yet, hives are tremendously complex and efficient systems. Anyone who disagrees needs only to leave out a cup of sugar-water for a day or two. Despite having limited intelligence, negligible communication abilities, a short lifespan, and minimal opportunity to develop experience, ants somehow coordinate a system involving thousands of actors in dynamic conditions to sustain the entire colony. They do it through *systematized chaos*.

Ants face a variety of threats. One particular species, *Temnothorax rugatulus*, live in crevices across the United States and Europe. Red and approximately a quarter of a centimeter long, their colonies are relatively small with between 50 to 150 ants. At some stage, whether it's through overpopulation or the clumsy interactions of an overly interested animal, the colony needs to move. Emigration is fraught with danger—colonize the wrong place and the colony is sure to be short-lived. The risk is tremendous.

In picking a new site, the ants face two major challenges. First, they are totally decentralized. With no controller to make decisions, there's no clear hierarchy nor coordination. Yet somehow, the colony needs to build consensus before it moves. That leads immediately to the second problem: ants are, sad to say, not very smart. They can communicate, but their vocabulary isn't big enough to have a measured debate.

Despite these limitations, these ants have evolved a tremendously efficient solution. Through a process called *quorum sensing* and the use of a few simple local rules, they coordinate what is otherwise a highly a complex and chaotic system to a new stable and relatively optimal equilibrium.

As soon as their nest cracks open, a small proportion of ants are sent out as scouts to hunt for a new nesting site. These scouts follow a few simple rules. They each set off in a direction different from their peers. As soon as they find a potential nest, they evaluate it based on a few criteria. They search for other dead ants, evaluate the size of the interior, and consider the number of openings as gauged by available light. After their evaluation is complete, they return to the now-unsafe nest and wait. If their potential nest was high quality, they wait a relatively short time. If they judged it to be of poor quality, they wait a relatively long time.

After waiting, they engage in "tandem running." They grab a partner and lead them to the potential site. This new scout also evaluates the site and makes up its own mind on whether it is high or low quality. They both then return to the original nest and, if the second ant considers the new site to be of a high enough quality, the process repeats with both ants waiting before recruiting new scouts. Otherwise, the second ant waits to be grabbed by a new partner or, failing that, sets off exploring on its own.

In a relatively short period of time, these scouts will probably inspect and compare multiple locations. More important, though, no single ant will likely see every location; comparisons are made on local experience, not global knowledge. Eventually, the best sites will see the greatest back-and-forth traffic. Because the ants that inspect that site wait the shortest period of time before recruiting other followers, the number of ants visiting the best available site will tend to increase the fastest.

At some stage, the proportion of ants visiting the best site exceeds an arbitrary threshold. At that point, they make a collective decision to move the entirety of the colony. Once a quorum has been achieved, they rapidly carry the brood, queen, and even other workers to the new nest. Scouts still searching are recruited through tandem running and merged into the collective.

Despite never making a global comparison of all potential sites, the colony makes a collective evaluation through local comparisons. By trusting the imperfect wisdom of crowds and a complex adaptive system governed by local rules, the colony rapidly makes the best decision it can in an efficient and relatively parsimonious manner. And, it does so despite lacking intelligence, communication skills, or even a central decision maker.

Coordinating the mass emigration of hundreds (or even thousands) of people without being able to speak, write, vote, or even make an official decision might seem impossible. And yet, through six simple rules, these ants do it effortlessly. To see how simple such a system can be, consider the following rules:

1. If the nest is destroyed, randomly nominate 20 percent of workers to be scouts.

2. Each scout should set off in a different direction for a maximum of five minutes.

3. On finding a potential site, give it a score between 1 and 10, taking into account security and size.

4. If maximum time has expired and no site has been found, return to the nest.

5. On returning to the nest, if a potential site has been found with a score of 9 or 10, immediately recruit a follower and return to the nest. If it had a score of 6 to 8, wait 30 seconds before recruiting a follower. If it had a score of 3 to 5, wait 2 minutes before recruiting a follower. If it had a score of less than 3, wait up to 5 minutes to be recruited. If, after those 5 minutes you have not been recruited, return to step 2 and repeat process.

6. If, on returning to the nest, you encounter more than 20 percent of the nominated scouts during your waiting period, follow them to the nominated site.

In classically hierarchical decision-making systems, processes become dependent on specific individuals. Broken links can derail everything. And yet, quorum sensing is entirely ant-independent; even if specific ants are eaten or otherwise lost, the colony will seamlessly adapt and find a way. It's a measure of how powerful this bottom-up approach to managing complexity and uncertainty is that it's evolved not only in ants but also bacteria, honeybees, and other social insects. In some ways, this distributed approach toward intelligence may even reflect the higher processing powers of more advanced evolutionary systems.[42]

Simple steps can give rise to surprisingly complex and robust systems.[43] The theory behind these systems has been around for decades. Often called *cellular automata* or *agent-based models*, they've been a solution looking for a problem.[44] In the *era of uncertainty* with its resulting complexity, their time has come.

This *systematized chaos* is a perfect example of how local rules and crowdsourcing can help manage the increasingly complex systems we are developing. And, lest one think that this is futurism at its finest, Amazon is already doing so to manage its highly complex supply chains.

In 1998, Amazon faced a crisis in its supply chain.[45] During an otherwise-ordinary Thanksgiving, Amazon faced one of the worst things a successful retailer can experience: more orders being placed than being shipped. In an "all-hands-on-deck" mandate, employees were required to work graveyard shifts across multiple warehouses, executives included.

One particularly bad backlog happened in Amazon's distribution center in Georgia. As unfulfilled orders continued to mount, the SWAT team finally identified the culprit: a missing pallet of Jigglypuffs, a toy from the Pokémon franchise. Amazon immediately mobilized a scouting team to find the missing pallet and they set off on their expedition. Hyperbole aside, this was no small task; it involved searching a 74,000-square-meter warehouse, an area roughly equivalent to almost 400 houses! It took three days to find but the lesson was invaluable: even the most complex and intelligent systems are useless when they're fragile.

Today, Amazon uses a system it's branded *chaotic storage*.[46] Classic warehousing systems involve having a fixed space for every product. Storage is managed through checking in and checking out products via barcodes or radio-frequency identifiers (RFID). Volumes are dynamic but position is static; the same products will always be located in the same place in the warehouse.

In relatively simple situations, this approach is easy to manage. Consider going shopping at the supermarket. While there's an entry cost in learning where everything is, once you know your way around it's easy and efficient to shop. The unfortunate trade-off is that to be efficient, every shopper needs to have the intelligence and experience to know the unique layout of the shop they're browsing. Otherwise, they lose products and need to go into a manual search, much like how Amazon's search teams needed to track down Jigglypuff.

As designed, this system offloads the complexity onto the individual. Without adequate training and experience, the system is only as strong as its weakest link. It also can't scale; what works well for a few hundred products on shelves in an area as large as a few houses becomes almost totally unmanageable when used in one of Amazon's gargantuan distribution center. If one can't find a tin of baked beans in the supermarket, it's simply a five-minute search. When it came to the missing pallet of Jigglypuffs, it was a three-day expedition.

Much like the ants, Amazon turned the model on its head. Rather than holding location static, Amazon made it dynamic. Both the product *and* the location would be scanned on receipt and fulfillment. Rather than place similar items together, packers would be free to place anything anywhere as long as they registered where they'd put it. By taking this approach, Amazon preserved the benefits of chaos but systematized it.

At any given point of time, an outside observer would have no hope of knowing where any given product would be at any point of time. For those inside the system though, the system works efficiently. Products held can be placed in the first available holding bay, giving the workers the opportunity to self-optimize. Finding any given package is easy through having access to the system that keeps track of what product was placed where. Rather than having to learn the system, new employees simply need to learn to follow simple instructions. The geography and landmarks are irrelevant; all that's important is learning the navigation system.

The system works. In 2010, Amazon picked and shipped 13 million items in 24 hours. In 2011, Amazon picked and shipped 17 million items, and this is across more than 80 different fulfillment centers globally.[47]

Complex and chaotic systems are inherently unmanageable. Top-down management approaches rarely work well; they are brittle and tend to collapse. Today and tomorrow's world is unlikely to become simpler. Instead, complexity will be the norm. Not only will organizations need to come to terms with uncertainty, but they'll also need to understand how best to leverage crowdsourcing and complex adaptive systems to systematize chaos.

NOTES

1. Alvin Toffler, *Future Shock* (New York: Random House, 1970).
2. Joseph S. Nye and John D. Donahue, *Governance in a Globalizing World* (Washington, DC: Visions of Governance for the 21st Century, 2000), 46.
3. John Gruber, "The iPhone 5S and 5C," *Daring Fireball*, September 17, 2013, http://daringfireball.net/2013/09/the_iphone_5s_and_5c (accessed Jan. 11, 2014).

4. Martin Hilbert, "When Is Cheap, Cheap Enough to Bridge the Digital Divide? Modeling Income Related Structural Challenges of Technology Diffusion in Latin America," *World Development* 38, no. 5 (2010): 756–770.

5. U.S. Census Bureau, "Computer and Internet Use in the United States," May 2013, www.census.gov/prod/2013pubs/p20-569.pdf.

6. Mauro F. Guillen and Sandra L. Suarez, "Explaining the Global Digital Divide: Economic, Political and Sociological Drivers of Cross-National Internet Use," *Social Forces* 84, no. 2 (2005): 681–708.

7. Wael Ghonim, *Revolution 2.0: The Power of the People Is Greater than the People in Power: A Memoir* (New York: Houghton Mifflin Harcourt, 2012).

8. Carsten Fink, Aaditya Mattoo, and Ileana Cristina Neagu, "Assessing the Impact of Communication Costs on International Trade," *Journal of International Economics* 67, no. 2 (2005): 428–445.

9. George Soros, "The Worst Market Crisis in 60 Years," *Financial Times*, Jan. 22, 2008, www.ft.com/cms/s/0/24f73610-c91e-11dc-9807-000077b07658.html?nclick_check=1 (accessed Jan. 11, 2014).

10. Nassim Nicholas Taleb, *The Black Swan: The Impact of the Highly Improbable* (New York: Random House, 2007).

11. Jean Piaget, *The Origins of Intelligence in Children* (New York: International Universities Press, 1952); and Jean Piaget, *The Construction of Reality in the Child* (New York: Basic Books, 1954).

12. P. Dasen, "Culture and Cognitive Development from a Piagetian Perspective," in W. J. Lonner and R. S. Malpass (eds.), *Psychology and Culture* (Boston: Allyn & Bacon, 1994).

13. Richard Dawkins, *The Selfish Gene* (New York: Oxford University Press, 1989).

14. "Doge," Know Your Meme, http://knowyourmeme.com/memes/doge (accessed Jan. 11, 2014).

15. G. E. Moore, "Cramming More Components Onto Integrated Circuits," *Proceedings of the IEEE* 86, no. 1 (1998): 82–85.

16. Chip Walter, "Kryder's Law," *Scientific American* (August 2005).

17. Megan Garber, "You Probably Write a Novel's Worth of Email Every Year," *The Atlantic*, Jan. 8, 2013, www.theatlantic.com/technology/archive/2013/01/you-probably-write-a-novels-worth-of-email-every-year/266942/ (accessed Jan. 12, 2014).

18. Matthew Finnegan, "Boeing 787s to Create Half a Terabyte of Data per Flight, Says Virgin Atlantic," *Computerworld* UK, Mar. 6, 2013, www.computerworlduk.com/news/infrastructure/3433595/boeing-787s-create-half-terabyte-of-data-per-flight-says-virgin-atlantic.

19. G. A. Akerlof, "The Market for Lemons: Quality Uncertainty and the Market Mechanism," *Quarterly Journal of Economics* 84, no. 3 (Aug. 1970): 488–500.

20. Vaclav Smil, *Prime Movers of Globalization: The History and Impact of Diesel Engines and Gas Turbines* (Cambridge, MA: MIT Press, 2010).

21. Evan Stubbs, *Delivering Business Analytics: Practical Guidelines for Best Practice* (Hoboken, NJ: John Wiley & Sons, 2013).

22. Thomas H. Davenport and Jeanne G. Harris, *Competing on Analytics: The New Science of Winning* (Boston: Harvard Business School, 2007).

23. "Salary/Income of Analytics/Data Mining/Data Science Professionals, *KDnuggets*, Feb. 2013, www.kdnuggets.com/2013/02/salary-analytics-data-mining-data-science-professionals.html (accessed Jan. 12, 2014).

24. Simon Miller, "Majority of Data and Analytics Industry Saw Pay Rise in 2012," Research-live.com, Oct. 4, 2013, www.research-live.com/news/news-headlines/majority-of-data-and-analytics-industry-saw-pay-rise-in-2012/4010571.article (accessed Jan. 12, 2014).

25. Annette Slunjski, "Results from IAPA Skills and Salary Survey," IAPA, Dec. 11, 2013, www.iapa.org.au/Article/ResultsFromIAPASkillsAndSalarySurvey (accessed Jan. 12, 2014).

26. Patrick Thibodeau, "Big Data to Create 1.9M IT Jobs in U.S. by 2015, Says Gartner," *Computerworld*, Oct. 22, 2012, www.computerworld.com/s/article/9232721/Big_data_to_create_1.9M_IT_jobs_in_U.S._by_2015_says_Gartner (accessed Jan. 12, 2014).

27. James Manyika, Michael Chui, Brad Brown, Jacques Bughin, Richard Dobbs, Charles Roxburgh, and Angela Hung Buyers, "Big Data: The Next Frontier for Innovation, Competition, and Productivity," McKinsey & Company, May 2011, www.mckinsey.com/insights/business_technology/big_data_the_next_frontier_for_innovation (accessed Jan. 12, 2014).

28. Malcolm Gladwell, *Outliers: The Story of Success* (New York: Little, Brown, 2008).

29. A. H. Maslow, "A Theory of Human Motivation," *Psychological Review* 50, no. 4 (1943): 370–396.

30. *The Derrick's Hand-book of Petroleum: A Complete Chronological and Statistical Review of Petroleum Developments* (Pittsburgh: Derrick Publishing Company, 1898).

31. Grant Segall, *John D. Rockefeller: Anointed with Oil* (New York: Oxford University Press, 2001).

32. BP, "Statistical Review of World Energy 2013," Jun. 2013, www.bp.com/en/global/corporate/about-bp/energy-economics/statistical-review-of-world-energy-2013.html (accessed Jan. 9, 2014).

33. Almanac of American Wealth, "The Richest Americans," *CNNMoney*, http://money.cnn.com/galleries/2007/fortune/0702/gallery.richestamericans.fortune/index.html (accessed Jan. 12, 2014).

34. Martyn McLaughlin, "New GTA V Release Tipped to Rake in £1bn in Sales," *The Scotsman*, Sept. 8, 2013, www.scotsman.com/lifestyle/technology/new-gta-v-release-tipped-to-rake-in-1bn-in-sales-1-3081943 (accessed Jan. 12, 2014).

35. Blake Snow, "Why Most People Don't Finish Video Games," CNN, Aug. 17, 2011, http://edition.cnn.com/2011/TECH/gaming.gadgets/08/17/finishing.videogames.snow (accessed Jan. 12, 2014).

36. Georg Zoeller, "Development Telemetry in Video Games Projects," GDC 2010, www.gdcvault.com/play/1012434/Development-Telemetry-in-Video-Games (accessed Jan. 9, 2014).

37. Clive Thompson, "Halo 3: How Microsoft Labs Invented a New Science of Play," *Wired.com*, Aug. 21, 2007, www.wired.com/gaming/virtualworlds/magazine/15-09/ff_halo?currentPage=all (accessed Jan. 12, 2014).

38. Graham Cluley, "LG Says It Will Push Out Firmware Update for Spy TVs, but Fails to Apologise," Nov. 21, 2013, http://grahamcluley.com/2013/11/lg-firmware-update-spy-tv/?utm_source=rss (accessed Jan. 12, 2014).

39. R. Menzel and Martin Giurfa, "Cognitive Architecture of a Mini-Grain: The Honeybee," *Trends in Cognitive Sciences* 5, no. 2 (Feb. 2001): 62.

40. Steven M. Platek, Julian Paul Keenan, and Todd K. Shackelford, *Evolutionary Cognitive Neuroscience* (Cambridge, MA: MIT Press, 2006).

41. Joel N. Shurkin, "When Ants Get Together to Make a Decision," *Inside Science*, Nov. 5, 2012, www.insidescience.org/content/when-ants-get-together-make-decision/834 (accessed Jan. 12, 2014).

42. Douglas R. Hofstadter, *Gödel, Escher, Bach: An Eternal Golden Braid* (New York: Basic Books, 1979).

43. Stephen Wolfram, *A New Kind of Science* (Wolfram Media, 2002).

44. Martin Gardner, "Mathematical Games: The Fantastic Combinations of John Conway's New Solitaire Game 'Life,'" *Scientific American* 223 (Oct. 1970): 120–123.

45. Gretchen Gavett, "How One Bad Thanksgiving Shaped Amazon," *Harvard Business Review*, Nov. 27, 2013, http://blogs.hbr.org/2013/11/how-one-bad-thanksgiving-shaped-amazon (accessed Jan. 12, 2014).

46. Rebecca Greenfield, "Inside the Method to Amazon's Beautiful Warehouse Madness: The Wire," Dec. 3, 2012, www.thewire.com/technology/2012/12/inside-method-amazons-beautiful-warehouse-madness/59563 (accessed Jan. 12, 2014).

47. The Whole Truth, "Amazon Boast Chaotic Storage System," Dec. 19, 2012, www.the-whole-truth.co.uk/chaotic-storage-system (accessed Jan. 12, 2014).

PART
TWO

Understanding Culture and Capability

t's interesting to note that many professionals talk of their business as "practices." Business analytics is similar. While best practices exist, there's no "end-game" as such.[1] Instead, it's all about being better. Innovation and differentiation come from improving in some way.

Business analytics is a discipline in every sense of the word. It's of limited value when treated as a series of ad hoc activities. Instead, scale requires structure and definition. It rarely drives competitive advantage when applied functionally and treated as a diversion. It requires focus and attention. And, it is rarely sustainable when it's treated as a "one-off." Real success comes from repeatability and reuse.

Getting all this right takes time. Some research suggests that establishing a new self-sustaining culture can take as long as five to seven years.[2] Still, every journey starts with a plan. Whether you're supporting or driving change, everything's impossible without knowing not only where the organization *is* but also where it needs to be. For most, building this understanding only comes with experience.

For someone with a deadline, that's probably somewhat disheartening. However, there's a shortcut. By learning from others, it's possible to bypass many of the dead ends that create delays. Why guess, when there are so many great examples out there?

Part Two describes two models to frame organizational transformation. Everything starts with culture and capability. Without the right capability, even the easiest things are impossible. Vision without the ability to execute is simply a good idea. Without the right culture, however, capability is meaningless. Being able to do something doesn't mean much if there's no interest in doing it.

Achieving real differentiation is impossible without both. As such, these models form the framework that describes how organizations harness their capabilities and use them to innovate. As shown in Figure P2.1, they affect how organizations create value from information. They affect how organizations create value from business analytics through *the value of business analytics*, as covered in Chapter 6. They affect how organizations treat their human capital through *the SMART model*, as covered in Chapter 7. And, they affect how organizations innovate through *the innovation engine*, as covered in Chapter 8.

The cultural imperative, covered in Chapter 3, focuses on the behaviors and attitudes of high-performing organizations. It outlines the five perspectives organizations go through on their way to differentiation through business analytics. At a minimum, every organization should aim to achieve at least the third level within this model. Anything less leads to inefficiencies, delays, and unacceptable risk.

The intelligent enterprise, covered in Chapter 4, focuses on the technical characteristics of organizations as they transition from chaos to the intelligent enterprise. It applies more to larger organizations, ones that are big enough to justify centralized technology infrastructure. For these organizations, anything less than the top level should be seen as underperforming.[3]

Together, they reflect an organization's ability to treat information as an active competitive differentiator rather than just a passive driver for better decision making.

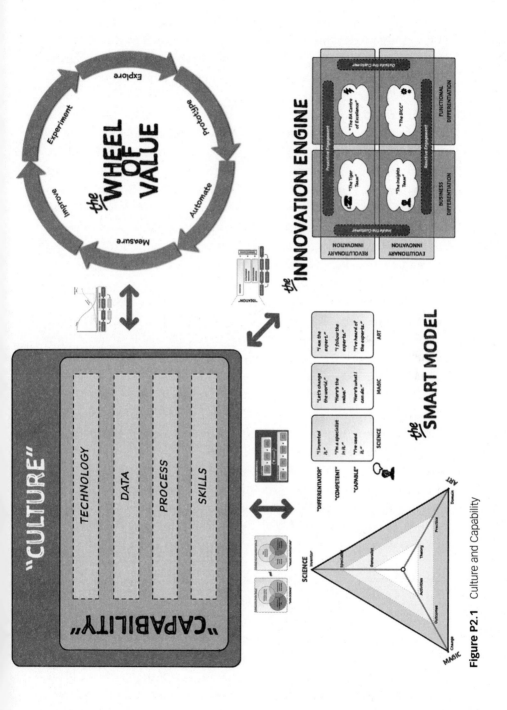

Figure P2.1 Culture and Capability

It's best to view these models as a set of guidelines. They describe direction and philosophy, not specific steps. As much as we'd like it to be, reality isn't black or white; it's a muddy mix of gray. Organizations are highly multidimensional and, more often than not, they're at multiple levels depending on the lens used.

For example, when viewed as a whole the dominant culture might be focused on insight rather than generating value. By this measure, the organization would be at the lowest level. Slice it by the IT group and it might look like a level-two organization due to a slightly higher level of warehousing maturity. Slice again by line of business and marketing might be sitting at the highest level due to a particularly visionary chief marketing officer and significant investment into customer-centric systems and management approaches. Shift across to finance, however, and it might drop back to level one because of hordes of spreadsheet jockeys.

Something these models don't comment on is technical proficiency. An organization can be very mature at managing technology or developing models while still being totally incapable of innovation or value creation. Data warehousing is a case in point—many organizations have mature, efficient, and highly scalable warehouses that are more than capable of handling "big data." However, many of those same organizations have no idea how to commercialize their data assets. As will become clearer in Chapter 7, technical skills are only one part of human capital. Equally, if not more important, are behaviors and a focus on value creation.

Getting better is an important goal. More important is making it stick. Achieving sustainable competitive advantage is a continuous endeavor and because of this, the goals will constantly shift. There is no finish line at which the team can pack up and go home.

This is good and bad. On one hand, it's tempting to give up. With no completion target, teams may become discouraged. On the other, it also means that there's no shortage of additional value that the team can generate—organizations are complex systems and their environment is constantly changing. There is *always* additional value that could be created.

Best practice doesn't mean perfection. Being perfect is an ideal, not reality. As such, the best approach is not to chase a particular level within either of these models. Instead, focus on what's important: creating value. Everything else, these models included, is just a way of getting there.

NOTES

1. See Evan Stubbs, *Delivering Business Analytics: Practical Guidelines for Best Practice* (Hoboken, NJ: John Wiley & Sons, 2013), Chapter 2.
2. John P. Kotter, *Leading Change* (Boston: Harvard Business Review, 2012).
3. This framework is a simplified version of the one presented in Chapter 3 of my previous book, *The Value of Business Analytics*. The top level in this book, "The Intelligent Enterprise," equates to the top three levels as described in my prior book. Where they are presented as discrete levels in my prior book, they are described as a continuum in this book.

The Cultural Imperative

There's an excellent passage in Pirsig's book, *Zen and the Art of Motorcycle Maintenance*, where he talks of the relative value of a screw.[1] Screws are cheap. They're so cheap that they're practically inconspicuous. When they're working, they're invisible. It's only when they don't that we care.

An interest in quality can emerge anywhere, even in repairing a motorcycle. At some stage, everyone has stripped a screw. Normally, it's just irritating. When that screw holds the engine compartment shut, though, its relative importance changes. It may have once been a 10-cent screw. Now, its value is roughly equivalent to the resale value of your bike; if you can't get that screw out, your bike is worthless. And with that epiphany, you've probably suddenly become very interested in screws.

Culture's the same. When culture's supportive, it's invisible. It's only when it's an inhibitor that we notice it. Analytics is possible without a supportive culture; every organization has largely disliked cowboys that it still values. *Business analytics*, however, is a different game. Value only comes from getting people to work together. That's only possible when people agree on what it is they're chasing.

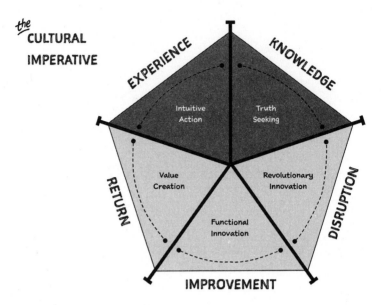

Figure 3.1 The Cultural Imperative

This chapter covers the *cultural imperative*, as shown in Figure 3.1. It describes the five perspectives on how information supports innovation and creates value.

Every organization exhibits one or more of these to varying degrees. At a minimum, effective organizations are comfortable with intuitive action and truth seeking. The most high-functioning organizations manage to balance all of these competing points of view into a cohesive whole, creating dynamic value (covered in Chapter 8). The most dysfunctional organizations tend to coalesce around one point of view, becoming blind to opportunity in their dogmatic pursuit of a single goal.

Not everyone need be a disruptor. Everyone, however, needs to understand that the best results come from being comfortable with multiple points of view.

INTUITIVE ACTION

Intuition is a powerful force. Our brain has greater processing power than the world's largest supercomputer. Its ability to detect patterns is unparalleled. Because of this, experience is an essential part of success—without it, all we do is continually rediscover known solutions, wasting time and effort. However, this doesn't mean that we *always* come to the right conclusion on experience alone.

Copious research has demonstrated that we're horrible when it comes to unexpected situations. Our brain takes shortcuts constantly, building patterns and hiding them from the conscious part of our decision-making processes. These patterns help us make snap decisions, ones that work more often than they fail. When these patterns are violated, however, our intuition usually leads us astray.

Organizations that build a monoculture around this perspective are challenging places to be. Above all else, they value *experience*. On the positive, they tend to place strong emphasis on rewarding internal success. Experience is recognized and promoted. Assuming the right person can be identified, decisions are often made quickly—experience trumps all.

However, there are negatives. Rather than running on facts, the business operates on opinions and conjecture. Because of the link between experience and seniority, the highest-paid person in the room usually controls direction regardless of how valid or justifiable his or her beliefs are. "Analytics" is sometimes a dirty word, assuming the organization even has the capability in the first place. Even when people *do* go to the effort of sourcing valid information, it's normally ignored.

Apart from the smallest of organizations, those that build a monoculture around this perspective only have two futures. Either they get better at using their information or they go bankrupt. The only exception is if they're protected or a de-facto monopoly; any other situation usually ends in ruin or improvement.

The Lost Manufacturer

One of the "best" examples I've seen of an organization that built a monoculture around this perspective was a manufacturer that blended local assembly with global sourcing. While they had complete control over local assembly, they were largely at the whim of their global suppliers when it came to importing foreign goods.

Admittedly, their business was not an easy one. Their internal politics meant that a shipping contract meant little in practice. While they might submit an order for 200 goods of a particular type, they'd often open the container three months later to discover they'd been shipped 100 goods of a different type. In other months, they'd find 500 goods. It's not easy running a global business when your partners can't hold up their end of the contract.

When I talked with them, they were struggling. Their supply chain was hurting them, but it was more than that. Sales were down. Customers were unhappy. Recalls were up. Their problems were numerous. However, one of their biggest problems was that the product they were landing on shore didn't match what the market wanted.

Every month, their stock on-hand kept increasing. Obviously, this hurt their cash-flow; the money they were spending on product was getting locked up in capital. However, the bigger problem was more insidious. Despite their best efforts, they just weren't importing what the public wanted. Every month their inventory kept getting bigger.

I met with their planning team to discuss how they might fix these problems. In the room were the people who designed, ordered, sold, and marketed their products. After watching them for 20 minutes, it was painfully clear that their problems weren't because of strategy or even execution. Quite simply, it was because they couldn't agree on what they were doing.

They disagreed about how many products they'd sold over the last quarter. They disagreed about how large their potential market was. They disagreed about what they should be selling. They disagreed about who their customers were. They even disagreed about whether things were dire.

An hour later, the only thing they'd agreed on was that they couldn't agree. We walked out of the room having decided nothing.

To their credit, some of the more forward-looking people tried to raise these fundamental issues with their leadership team. Unfortunately, they were resoundingly shut down; those making the decisions were unquestionable. With over 20 years' experience, the data was quite simply irrelevant. In the battle between gut-feel and evidence, experience always trumped reality.

Three years later, they declared bankruptcy. Their local operations downsized by over 60 percent during the restructuring. And, despite a last-minute bailout from an interested party, their long-run sustainability is still in question. Their challenges were many and their successes few. However, one of their biggest blind spots was simply a complete and total resistance to actually *using* their information to support better decision making.

Common Characteristics

Organizations that revolve around this perspective often lurch from bad decision to bad decision. They have little understanding of how to define, manage, or even use information effectively. Because of this, decisions are made not on weight of evidence but on force of personality. Sometimes, through sheer serendipity, they get it right. Unfortunately, that single success usually justifies years of subsequent failures.

Culture doesn't magically appear. At some point, it was created because of its environment. Because of this, it's hard to fault their reliance on experience over evidence. More often than not, their data is usually fragmented, of highly variable quality, and generally not trustworthy. Usually, their culture was created by this very lack of information. However, this doesn't forgive *perpetuating* a dysfunctional culture. As this culture becomes the dominant one, they progressively ignore the root cause of their bad data: their own behaviors.

Analytics is seen as either being "too hard" or outright untrustworthy. If the data contradicts popular opinion, the default position is that the data is incorrect. Results are cherry-picked to support particular positions. In any given meeting, a substantial proportion of time is usually spent arguing what the right numbers are.

The almost total absence of data-driven decision making creates a vicious cycle. Decisions are made in the absence of data. When the organization acts on these decisions, this same lack of data makes it impossible to measure the effectiveness of those decisions. Because there's no traceability, everyone claims credit for successes and disowns failures. The successes people are happy to acknowledge justify the power of pure experience-based decision making. Because failures are ignored or outright covered up, this biased view ends up reinforcing the dominant culture.

Ironically, everyone normally agrees that things should be better. Sadly, the dominant culture prevents anyone from actually doing anything differently. And so, while things are obviously not as effective as they could be, the status quo remains.

Being comfortable with this perspective does have advantages:

- **Egalitarianism.** Success and internal experience is valued above all. Whether it's through experience or intuition, those who succeed are frequently promoted to positions of power and influence.

- **Clarity of ownership.** Sources of power are centralized and either explicitly or tacitly understood. Decisions rarely rely on consensus—specific individuals often have sole decision-making capability due to their experience. While they may or may not consult, they will eventually rely on their intuition taking into account the information presented to them.

- **Trust.** Those with the authority to make decisions are conferred a high degree of trust by the leadership team of the organization. This often encourages self-determination, personal responsibility, and the ability for individual units within the organization to operate semi-autonomously.

However, it does come with disadvantages. Some indicators of an organization excessively grounded in this perspective are:

- **HiPPO leadership.** The data people need to make their decisions either doesn't exist or isn't trusted. Analytics is rarely (if ever) applied. Subjectivity and gut-feel is the standard operating model, usually dictated by the *highest-paid person's opinion*.

- **Unconsidered reaction.** Firefighting is common and decisions are made without any clarity on how their effectiveness will be measured. Knee-jerk reactions are common and while plans may be made, they're rarely held to.

- **Fragmented inconsistency.** Decisions are made without consideration of their broader impacts. Outcomes are rarely (if ever) measured, making it impossible to understand what's working and what isn't. Fiefdoms abound and decisions are made on self-interest rather than based on organizational objectives.

- **Self-delusion and outright denial.** Successes are claimed by all. Failures, however, are ignored or outright covered up, preventing valuable learning.

- **Survival.** The most common measure of success is treading water and simply maintaining the status quo. Achieving this is "good enough." Change is often seen as an active threat.

- **Aimless direction.** Key performance indicators are undefined and tenure is determined by politics rather than merit. Success is a subjective measure doled out by management based on unclear criteria.

- **Frantic desperation.** People constantly reinvent their job every time they face a challenge. Inputs and outputs are undefined and when employee turnover happens, business processes are reinvented from scratch.

- **Person-centricity.** Competencies are not recognized, acknowledged, or even understood. Making something happen inevitably involves contacting a specific individual, without which everything becomes impossible.

- **Incapacitated and paralyzed.** Good ideas are ignored because of fundamental gaps in capability. Rather than being seen as an opportunity to improve, these gaps are used as a crutch to justify stagnation and the rejection of change.

- **Problem-based debate.** Cross-functional and internal disagreements are totally subjective in nature and focus on the root cause of current issues. Different parties will attribute current challenges to different sources, and rather than look for solutions, they'll argue about causes with no clear path to resolution. Usually ending at loggerheads, the different groups will take independent (and sometimes conflicting) actions to solve what they feel is "the real issue."

- **Feudal artisans.** Skills are hoarded by manual craftspeople who have developed their experience through years of practical application. The political enterprise guards their skills through the creation of fiefdoms and leverages their unique capabilities for internal political gain.

■ **Technology is "nice to have."** Despite missing fundamental capabilities, technology is seen as a "nice-to-have" and is heavily neglected in favor of hiring and developing artisans. Spreadsheets multiply and information is a closely guarded power base for those who have accumulated it.

Expanding the Culture

Too much of one thing is rarely healthy. For most organizations with a monoculture of intuitive action, eventually things get so bad that something has to change. Their usual solution is very data-centric. If the problem is that they don't have good data, the answer must be to get that data. They decide that they need to consolidate, standardize, and cleanse all their information. Usually, they run out and buy a warehouse, appliance, or other storage platform and embark on a large-scale data transformation project.

Intuitively, this makes a lot of sense. This isn't entirely wrong, either. It's critical that every organization have access to high-quality information. It's just that it's not the whole picture. While it's an essential part of a functioning business analytics platform, it also unfortunately drives little value in isolation. It's what they *do* with the data that creates value.

Culturally, this usually marks the point where organizations become self-aware. They realize that even though they're highly experienced, they have an information problem and they need to fix it. Unfortunately, it's also where they often make a big mistake. After what's usually a very expensive and lengthy warehousing project, they realize that they have no idea what to do with the information they've consolidated.

On the positive side, they do normally get *some* productivity benefits. Standard measures usually enable some degree of operational efficiency and better performance measurement. On the negative side, this sudden deluge of information usually leads to "analysis paralysis." Despite knowing they have the data, they have no idea how to analyze it or even what to do with it.

Expanding the culture often involves getting people to acknowledge that accurate information (beyond financial measures) is critical to business success. Unfortunately, this means going directly against the dominant culture. Because of this, organizations with this monoculture usually only develop when faced with a "life-or-death" threat. Without that threat, "good enough" is good enough.

TRUTH SEEKING

Experience only ever goes so far. That which we know is dwarfed by that which we don't. When dealing with the unknown, the best course of action is usually research. Organizations that are comfortable with this perspective understand that information is a key source of value as long as it's effectively analyzed.

However, this isn't to say that truth seeking is inherently better than intuitive action. Organizations that build too much of a monoculture around truth seeking are often slower than their competitors in action and time to market. Above all else, they value *knowledge*. Everything needs to be exhaustively justified with empirical information before anyone is willing to act. Decisions require consensus based on deep validation of the evidence. Experience and intuition takes a back seat to analysis and because of this, conservatism usually reigns.

Balancing this with a perspective that understands intuitive action leads to better outcomes. Organizations that embrace *both* of these perspectives are hopeful, if often stressed. One of their defining characteristics is that regardless of what they say publicly, they know internally that they have problems. Of these, their biggest is often that they struggle to link big data and big data analytics to tangible returns. While they spend money, they're not entirely sure what it was worth.

They're often very advanced in many other ways. Their warehouses and reporting platforms may be technically excellent. Their operational processes may be extremely robust. They may even have very mature training and development programs. But, if you ask behind closed doors the tangible value of these, they'll usually acknowledge that it's hard to measure the returns. They'll have no problems telling you what their marketing campaigns are worth, but as to their data assets or the analysis they put into their data, your guess will probably be as good as theirs.

This isn't because they don't understand technology. Usually, it's because they place heavy emphasis on insight rather than outcomes. Their focus tends toward activities and tools and rather than being good at business analytics, they're experts in business intelligence or analytics. Many of their challenges lie in the way they view analysis— rather than seeing it as a discipline in its own right, they usually see it as something that can be solved by technology alone. This perspective actively undermines their long-term success.

Rise of the Technocrats

At one point, I was engaged by an organization to help with a technology selection process. They had unknowingly built a very strong monoculture around this perspective. Their main goal was to try to find the best technology they could to support customer matching. At our kickoff, 20 minutes into the conversation it was painfully obvious why they were struggling to connect with their customers in any meaningful way—they had absolutely no idea what their customers were interested in.

They had three separate sources of customer information across the group. One covered outbound communication, one services delivery, and one loyalty membership. For a variety of reasons they had never linked the three. In principle, they knew their customers' sociodemographic information, the households their customers were a part of, their spending over the last few years, the types of services they were most interested in, as well as their preferred communication channels. In practice, they could barely create a single clean list of email addresses.

Starting out with a single view of customer made a good deal of sense. The problem was that they hadn't thought about what should come next. They had no plans beyond creating a single view of customer—their implicit assumption was that by linking all their data, they'd somehow magically drive better customer engagement. When probed, there was no real engagement strategy. Despite having access to tremendously valuable behavioral and wealth information, their plans stopped at having a single source of truth and finding the "right" action. In many ways, they had the classic "if you build it, they will come" strategy. Unfortunately, their business case was based on a *big* revenue uplift through simply having this single view of customer.

I tried to explain that without the "what's next," it was unlikely that they'd deliver their proposed business case. There was nothing wrong with their desire to create a single view of customer. Nor was there anything wrong with the deep analysis they wanted to do. Their major problem was that they didn't know what they were trying to *do* with it. Having a single view of customer was an enabler, not an outcome. Their real challenge was working out how to leverage it once they had it, not how to create it in the first place.

The elephant in the room was that getting to that point would require a frank and objective review of how they went about acting on insights. Their real problem wasn't matching information; it was how they'd act on insight. Solving that problem would have required them to go back and redefine what they were trying to achieve based on the outcomes they wanted to drive rather than the technologies they wanted to buy.

Rather unsurprisingly, this was received rather poorly. They soundly rejected that point of view, firmly believing that by buying the right technologies their problems would disappear. Rather than looking into the skills, human capital, and processes they would need to develop, they wanted to focus on fuzzy matching routines and logical data architectures. They were so far down one track of thinking that nothing could persuade them otherwise.

At that point, I politely declined the offer to be engaged to deliver the project—it was painfully obvious that their project would likely fail and they would be looking for a scapegoat when things went badly. A year later, they had a great platform but still had yet to deliver any real outcomes. Shortly after that most of the team left for greener pastures.

Common Characteristics

Organizations with this perspective *love* technology and analysis. They're usually exceedingly good at buying it and managing it. They may also be experts in managing large-scale programs of work. Unfortunately, they also underestimate the importance of people, process, and data in driving change. Because of this, they're constantly surprised when their projects deliver less business value than they were expecting.

People often work to activities, not necessarily outcomes. They're often extremely good at using data to find answers to hard problems. They may also be experts in using their technology assets. When it comes to acting on that insight, however, they're less consistent. The answers they find have a tendency to either disappear or be diluted. Creating knowledge and answering questions is counted as success; no one looks to see whether that knowledge created any value.

These organizations almost always conflate analytics with business analytics. It's not that they're ignorant—they'll often "talk the talk" and say all the right things. In their mind, though, "business analytics" is about data mining, visualization, machine learning, and other functional capabilities. Because of this they're mainly interested in functionality and analytical asset creation. Model accuracy is more often than not the primary benchmark for quality. Once they hit a sufficient level of quality or find a deeper truth, their job is done.

What happens from there is less of a concern. How that knowledge was *used* to drive value is either irrelevant or overlooked. Typically, the teams responsible for analytics or business intelligence claim that that's someone else's job and their role is just to create insight. Virtually no attention is paid to change management and it's taken as a given that the organization should value the insights they produce. Because of this, the rest of the business often gets frustrated and either complains, recruits their own analysts, or outright gives up and gets on with their job.

Processes are usually undefined and rarely reused. While frequently intelligent and highly capable, their teams are collections of individuals. Cottage industries abound and almost everyone in the team does what they prefer rather than what's the most efficient. This lack of reuse carries across to data as well; the amount of analytical data duplication (and corresponding effort) in these organizations can be staggering at times. While they may claim multiple petabytes of analytical data, peel back the layers and often they may have only terabytes of core data. The gap between the two is simply data being duplicated by different people.

Without changing their perspective, these organizations rarely achieve any real form of repeatable value from business analytics. They have deep insight but frequently deliver business-as-usual outcomes. Differentiation is transitory and regression to the mean is the norm.

Embracing this perspective does have advantages:

- **Clarity of insight.** There is tremendous value in being able to use data to answer hard questions. Where intuition and experience end, analytics sometimes continues.

- **Experimental innovation.** The constant drive to extract progressive insight from information often leads to testing and applying radically innovative techniques.

- **Analytical creativity.** The breadth and depth of information sources under analysis usually reinforces a culture of continuous creativity, encouraging analysts to always ask "what if."

Indicators of an organization overly grounded in truth seeking at the expense of the other perspectives are:

- **Intelligent inaction.** While the organization has the capability to find answers from data, insights are rarely acted on and disappear into the ether. Despite the capacity for intelligence, the organization rarely uses it to its advantage. Often, the organization becomes trapped by "analysis paralysis," which is struggling with the cognitive dissonance of having *too much* information.

- **Considered reaction.** Firefighting declines in favor of planned tactical execution but strategic planning still presents a challenge.

- **Inward-looking.** As external measures are still too hard to track effectively, decisions are made based on convenience, internal satisfaction, and political consensus, not necessarily on what would most benefit the customer.

- **Internal value.** While analytics is applied, it's unclear how much economic value it adds to the bottom line. Success is gauged based on internal customer satisfaction, perceived productivity improvements, and ease of decision making. Projects are still seen as successful in the absence of tangible value as long as they make it easier to run the business.

- **Being the underdog.** The dominant culture is one focused on keeping up and beating the odds. Passion is strong but there's a tacit awareness that capability lags comparable organizations.

- **Activity targeting.** Performance management happens but is focused on activity. For example, marketing groups benchmark based on campaign volumes, not profitability. Service centers focus on working to their measures, not necessarily what's seen as valuable by their customers. Centralized business intelligence teams are often viewed with distrust or resentment by other areas of the business because of their lack of interest on the outcomes their customers are trying to drive.

- **Challenging delivery.** Success happens, albeit through heroic effort. Analytically related activities take orders of magnitude longer than better-performing peers.

- **Process-centricity.** Focus shifts from the person to the process. Ability, efficiency, and quality vary significant between processes but the business still develops points of understood engagement. Corporate memory develops to the point where processes and services remain consistent even if people and delivery approaches change over time.

- **Underutilized capability.** Investment into technology increases but gaps prevail. Technology selection is based on functionality and perceived need rather than defined by outcomes and tangible measures. Despite this investment into technology, the business has little understanding how to leverage it to create advantage.

- **Fact-based debate.** Data is captured and distributed but seen as confusing. Decision makers actively use data but frequently disagree as their data is heavily duplicated and somewhat inconsistent. Disagreements focus on measures and often lead to inaction because of an inability to agree on the *what*. Sanity often prevails but at the expense of delay and political friction.

- **Cottage industries.** Individuals, rather than teams, are the primary engagement point for specific knowledge or skills. Fiefdoms and feudal empires still exist but carry less weight; skills are recognized and in demand across business units. Power migrates from the chief to the craftsperson. As the gatekeeper to skills, he or she is highly valued but creates a significant bottleneck.

- **Technology is the answer.** Gaps are recognized, and investment is channeled to remedy gaps. Unfortunately, little is considered outside technology; acquisition is seen as a silver bullet and people, process, and change complexities are often ignored or severely underestimated. Information ceases to be a power base. In its stead it leaves overwhelming confusion due to an overabundance of undirected and unfocused capability.

Expanding the Culture

Organizations comfortable with truth seeking and intuitive action are usually in equilibrium. They understand the importance of data, even if they're not especially good at using it. They value insight, even if they don't always act on it. It may not be optimal, it may not even be efficient, but it's sustainable.

Faced with a problem, the answer these organizations leap to is almost always technology. If they don't have the experience and they can't get any insights from their data, the answer *must* be better tools. They end up doing an exhaustive search to select best-of-breed technology. They conduct exhaustive feature or function comparisons. They debate the relative merits of different algorithms, architectures, and processing paradigms. Unfortunately, all too often they neglect to ask the most important question of all: How am I going to use these new capabilities?

In the absence of knowing where the value will come from, the "build it and they will come" plan is only partly effective. Capability without intent is usually just needless structural cost. When it comes to their ability to use their information to create value, they're competitive if not necessarily innovative. As long as they can demonstrate innovation or differentiation elsewhere in the business, this culture perpetuates. There's a significant opportunity cost, but at least they don't go out of business.

Many organizations never move past this point. They stay in a holding pattern, generally frustrated and stressed but still delivering to business as usual. Getting past this point involves realizing that business analytics is about more than assets or technology. It's about value creation, change management, and innovation.

Many organizations have a dominant culture that reflects characteristics of both intuitive action and truth seeking. Unfortunately, these alone usually inhibit an organization's ability to generate significant or renewable return from big data and business analytics. Organizations that stop with these perspectives usually add cost to their business without any clearly measurable benefits.

Developing culture beyond this point rarely happens organically. Usually, it only happens when one of three things occurs. The first is total erosion of competitive differentiation. Whether it's through competitive catch-up or internal failure, the organization might see its core source of differentiation disappear. An organization known for customer satisfaction might find its market growth under threat if one of its competitors achieves equivalent levels of satisfaction. This search for a new source of differentiation can act as a trigger to approach business analytics and data-driven innovation differently.

The second is the introduction of one or more senior change agents. Whether it's through a board or executive leadership change, "new blood" may bring with them an understanding of the value of business analytics. Given the right senior support, this can act as a trigger to embark on cultural change.

The third is aspirational exposure. Many organizations look not only toward their competitors for inspiration but also outside of their industry sector. Whether it's through study tours, joint leadership planning sessions, or simply a conversation over the golf course, the existing leadership team may be exposed to an approach they'd like their organization to aspire to. This desire for improvement can then act as a trigger to push the boundaries of the organization's existing culture.

In the absence of these, there's no sense of urgency or reason to change. And without a reason, the status quo remains just that.

VALUE CREATION

Organizations comfortable with this perspective start realizing tangible value from business analytics. By chance or choice they've discovered that success stems from following repeatable processes and helping the organization to change. They believe it's about *value and outcomes* and, like a well-tuned machine, they bring together the business, IT, and the analysts into a coordinated team focused on value creation. Above all else, they look for *return*. While they can't *always* measure the value they create through their use of business analytics, they know they need to do it. And, more often than not, they do. Rather than focusing on insight, they try to directly link their analysis to measurable results.

They still care about sophistication of analysis and efficiency of algorithms. However, their primary goal is on the outcomes they're trying to drive. This focus on value creation carries across into how they manage performance, define roles, and task people. Even more More important, they understand that insight without action is worthless. People are actively encouraged to consider *impact* as success, not just *activity*.

They understand that without getting the rest of the organization to trust their results, everything they do is wasted. Because of this, they place specific emphasis on assisting front-of-house staff to leverage insights to drive measurable outcomes. They may not yet be at a point where business analytics is a core differentiator. However, they'll usually have a growing number of champions who see business analytics as a validated way of driving better business results.

Ironically, the biggest risk for organizations that embrace this perspective leads to stagnation. Despite having achieved real success, they'll usually start to falter without a well-defined roadmap. There is the constant risk that the competencies they've created will end up being constrained by the processes they've built.

In the worst case, the original innovators become consumed by business as usual. They get frustrated because they can't innovate, and eventually leave. Over time, the organization's competitive differentiation erodes and it's eventually left carrying significant overhead for no real competitive advantage. Like the wolf, regression to the mean is always knocking at the door.

The Unfortunate Regression

Organizations that understand this perspective see real value. Unfortunately, many also see real losses if they lose it. Over the course of a few years, one organization followed this precise trajectory. They started with a tremendously strong culture. They were a pleasure to work with, even being acknowledged by the broader market as "the place to be." Their enthusiasm levels were high, they had the explicit commitment of their chief marketing officer, and even better, they were rolling off the tail-end of a successful targeted marketing project. The head of their analytics team was a visionary with a strong sense of pragmatism who, through phenomenal effort and persuasion, had managed to successfully change their approach to direct marketing.

Prior to his joining the organization, the product teams were strong believers in the spray-and-pray school of marketing. Their conversion rates were so low that in order to hit their sales targets, they sent offers to *everyone*. With only minor exaggeration, it was so bad that their exclusion rules were, "If they're a customer, don't already have the product, and they're not dead, send the offer." This third requirement was only added *after* the campaigns had gone live (for obvious reasons).

This approach was tremendously inefficient, not to mention annoying to their customer base. For a purportedly customer-centric organization, they treated every single one of their customers exactly the same. Unsurprisingly, their churn rates at the time were among the highest in the market. While they didn't measure net promoter score, some informal focus group testing had indicated that the single highest factor in a customer's decision to churn was whether they'd recently spoken to the company in question. Things were bad.

Shortly after joining, this visionary analytics manager made it a high priority to augment their existing direct marketing activities with analytically based insight. To build the information base he needed, his first project was to create a single view of customer blended with behavioral information. However, he understood that this was a step, not the goal. By placing an emphasis on change management and persuasion, he also managed to convince the direct marketing team to change their approach. Rather than maintain the status quo, they would trial a champion/challenger approach and benchmark their existing targeting strategy against one based on customer segmentation combined with propensity models.

Getting to this point took months, but it was worth it. Where their existing conversion rates had been sitting at around 1 percent, the new approach had conversion rates of over 10 percent.* Even better, he

---

*A conversion rate is the proportion of offers sent that are acted on. A conversion rate of 1 percent would mean that for every 100 offers sent, only one would be acted on.

had managed to reduce the total number of offers going out (reducing marketing costs) while simultaneously beating the absolute number of offers accepted compared against their existing processes.

Whether through experience or luck, he had succeeded. And by doing so, he was able to demonstrate the value of business analytics in a very measurable and tangible way. Based on these results, the organization made a substantial investment in establishing a dedicated analytical marketing platform. They gave him the authority and investment needed to acquire the technologies and skills needed to take them to the next level.

Had their story ended at this point, they could have remained a case study in excellence. Unfortunately, they also became a case study in how easily things regress without constant attention. After a number of years of progressive success, that same visionary manager was offered an external higher profile position. Much to the organization's dismay, he accepted the offer and moved on. Even though this left a huge gap in their capability, it shouldn't have been enough to derail their focus. Before he left, he'd defined a strong roadmap with a series of clearly defined deliverables supported by a manageable cadence of initiatives. He'd created a culture that, in isolation, should have been self-sustaining.

The straw that broke the proverbial camel's back was his replacement. Despite being highly competent, he lacked the same degree of vision and persuasion. To establish his ownership over the role, one of the first things he did was to cancel the existing program of work under the guise of defining a better vision. This vision never eventuated and, over time, the team regressed to focusing only on maintaining what they had already delivered. Conversion rates were still high but nothing new was being delivered. Eventually, his team became bored and started to suffer high levels of staff attrition.

Over the course of the next three years the organization's competitors progressively caught up. Eventually, they overtook the organization. Almost on a monthly basis they saw their conversion rates decline back toward their original levels as their competitors became smarter with their marketing and their customers became more sophisticated. What had started out as a point of competitive differentiation was never converted into a source of ongoing competitive advantage. And, by failing to do so, their successes were short-lived. Where they should have created a culture of *revolutionary disruptor*, they instead regressed back to the mean by standing still.

Common Characteristics

Organizations with this perspective have a strong understanding of how their information is converted into insight. More importantly, they can quantify the value of this insight as it's acted on. They operate with a firm belief in the importance of action. Still, they often struggle with efficiency—many of their processes lack standardization, and they often make inconsistent use of automation.

They see tools as an essential but relatively unimportant piece of the picture. It's not that they don't appreciate the need for effective technology. It's just that they see it as necessary rather than sufficient.

They understand that the real challenges lie in change management and cultural transformation. Their leaders spend the majority of their time driving change and ensuring good processes are followed and relatively little time being directly involved in insight generation or other technical activities. While they have data scientists and other analysts, they understand the importance of role separation and believe that it's about far more than insights, data mining, or sheer sophistication. Instead, their analytics teams play a direct and involved role in making sure other business units apply their insights. Sometimes, this even goes so far as to take a supporting role in project delivery and field training.

While processes are often still fairly poorly defined, organizations demonstrating this perspective tend to be quite effective in reusing analytical data. Virtually all have established an analytical datamart of some form that promotes the centralization and reuse of data. More importantly, they don't do this because of an IT drive for storage rationalization; they do it because they believe it's the right thing to do. Teams act as coordinated groups and are actively interested in sharing their successes and efficiencies, even if there's usually no easy way of replicating them without effort and time.

The biggest challenges these organization face are usually around improving efficiency and justifying further investment. Despite being able to demonstrate success and measure value, they usually have a relatively weak grip on how any specific activities within their overall value chain contributed to those same successes. They still spend more time than they should managing data and not as much time as they should ensuring their existing assets are performing as well as they could be. Their ability to "build" is usually higher than their ability to "deploy-and-maintain." While they can turn around a new model fairly quickly, migrating it into production involves a great deal of frustration and delay.

These challenges limit the time they have for innovation. And because of this, they often find it difficult to drive economies of scope through reusing their now-mature skills to solve other problems across the organization. While their enthusiasm and experience is high, they simply don't have the time to expand their scope of operations in any meaningful way. As strong as they are on creating value, they still lag in terms of innovation.

Some indicators of organizations comfortable with this perspective are:

- **Intelligent action.** Insights are developed *and* acted on in a consistent manner. Information is used to generate advantage as a matter of course.

- **Considered planning.** Tactical outcomes are balanced against strategic objectives. This dual focus becomes pervasive; shared services teams focus more on the outcome than the asset and, because of this, are often viewed favorably by the business. However, deployment processes are still largely undefined. Every automation attempt takes a great deal of effort, involves uncertainty, and experiences delays.

- **Outward-looking.** External measures are monitored and decisions are made based on expected value. The customers' opinion and their resultant action is the central consideration in decision making.

- **External value.** Insights are acted on and drive measurable outcomes within specific operational processes. There are clear and well-defined linkages between intellectual assets (such as data, models, or processes) and tangible outcomes. Business analytics initiatives are funded based on well-defined business cases that identify (and eventually deliver) specific tangible returns.

- **Being competitive.** The dominant culture is one focused on being smarter than the market. It takes the organization substantially less time to create value from information than its competitors.

- **Outcome targeting.** Performance management happens and is focused on outcomes. Success measures are geared toward tangible value, even if specific measures vary across the organization.

- **Meeting the benchmark.** Focus shifts from capabilities and heroism to achieving parity with leading practices. Analytically related activities are comparable to intelligent peers.

- **Role-centricity.** Focus shifts from the process to the role. Capability, efficiency, and quality become consistent between processes and knowledge is shared between individuals. Requirements and activities are well defined, if not always tremendously efficient. Inputs, outputs, and all stages in between are documented and consistent between people. Analytical asset creation processes are repeatable and efficient.

- **Realized capability.** The business has developed an understanding of how to leverage technology to create advantage. Capability ceases to be an inhibitor and instead becomes an enabler and opportunity.

- **Action-based debate.** Analytical data is centralized and there is a high degree of reuse, even if this data is not necessarily stored in the most efficient format. Decision makers spend little time debating data and easily isolate quality issues if they occur. Disagreement instead focuses on what action should be taken for a given problem.

- **Scalable factories.** Teams are seen as the primary engagement point for specific knowledge or skill. Employee turnover slows the team down but does not derail it. Competencies are held by the team and the loss of one person has a manageable impact on the group. Fiefdoms and feudal empires disappear in favor of shared service centers and communities of practice. Knowledge is freely shared and scalable efficiency becomes valued over personal power. Power migrates from the craftsperson to those capable of enabling the broader business.

■ **Technology is an enabler.** Tools have been largely standardized within teams and are treated as a given. Rather than being seen as a silver bullet, technology is seen as just another dimension in an overall change process. Discussion about technology focuses on how it will create value, not on what functions it offers.

Expanding the Culture

Organizations that have hit this point understand how they *should* be managing. It's just that they don't always do it as consistently as they could. Their focus is usually on making sure they apply their new-found knowledge. While they don't always have a firm grasp on the details, they know they need to build a better understanding of how to apply business analytics if they're to see sustained return.

It's in adopting and applying this perspective where organizations start seeing real tangible returns from their investments. The shift in focus from internal to external value is an inflection point in their ability to generate value from their data. Naturally, this assumes they're successful—having the right vision is only part of the cultural imperative.

It is, however, just one more perspective. Expanding past this point is a case of change management. The people generating returns need to build a strong coalition of the willing, a broader group of interested parties who *also* believe in the value of business analytics. Transformation is key; jointly, their goal is a small (if still significant) change in their organization's business model.

FUNCTIONAL INNOVATION

Organizations with this perspective have extended their focus from one-off benefits to continual improvement. They've embraced the journey it implies and actively chase *functional innovation*. They understand how their business works, have the ability to measure it, and relentlessly search for and deliver continuous gains. Above all else, they value *improvement*.

To avoid the tightening labor market, these organizations put an emphasis on automation. They embed analytics within operational

microdecisions, improving decision quality as well as decision efficiency.[2] To ensure their analytical assets are effective, they've embraced
formal asset management and value measurement. To drive repeatability and process efficiency, they've standardized their processes and
minimized transaction costs through effective use of workflows. Tying
all this together is a series of key performance indicators that reinforce
positive behaviors and discourage inappropriate behaviors, supported
by a measurement framework that makes outcomes transparent.

Processes are well defined, roles and responsibilities clear, and
objectives transparent. New hires often find this disconcerting—
rather than having to operate independently, they often find there are
entire teams there to support them with analytical data management,
model operationalization, or any other number of specific competencies. The organization has well-defined structures to share information and cross-pollinate innovations. Even better, these structures are
actively used.

More than just looking for outcomes, they look for repeatability
and reuse. Economies of scale and scope become real and provide cost
advantages over their competitors. Quality and agility become more
than concepts; organizations at this level deeply understand and have
the ability to track, measure, and improve both. Embracing this perspective is a significant step; few organizations truly reach this point.
Those that do, have the sophistication and management maturity to
operate and coordinate truly complex management structures.

Moving beyond this point involves a clear executive commitment
to deliver sustainable competitive advantage through more than just
functionally aligned or efficient activities. Instead, the leadership team
must decide to treat business analytics as a differentiator in its own
right and embrace disruption. There is nothing to say that this is a
necessary step; many organizations look for differentiation elsewhere.
However, organizations that reach this or the next level create a form
of differentiation that, if sustained, is hard to replicate.

The Benefits of Being Personal

It takes a great deal of work to turn this perspective into part of the
dominant culture. Surprisingly, it can also take less time than one

might suppose. It just takes focus, an understanding of what's possible, and the commitment to get there.

Different organizations start their journey for different reasons. GE, for example, embarked on an exhaustive Six Sigma exercise to establish a level of quality and cost differentiation over their competitors. More than just a project, this became a major part of their culture. The benefits of getting to this level of focus are significant; Motorola, for example, credited the same approach with more than $17 billion of savings as of 2006.

Other organizations look to achieve success through analytical efficiency. They create "model factories," performance engines designed to automate the creation of analytical assets. In one case, an organization was able to reduce the time it took to define, create, and deploy their analytical assets to less than three days. This innovation though hyper-specialization gave them a significant advantage in their market.

Still others look to innovate through constant improvement. One such organization started with a focus on improving customer relationships. Like most organizations, they invested far more in trying to make the next sale than they did in servicing the customer's needs. To hit their sales targets, they rolled out an integrated marketing platform that allowed them to communicate across multiple channels. In less technical terms, they could pick up the same conversation with the customer across web, email, SMS, or phone.

While they'd been quite good at using analytics to refine their targeting strategies, this introduced a whole extra level of complexity. Not only did they have to take into account what a potential customer might be interested in but they had to factor in whether the customer liked being sold to over that channel. Undaunted, they innovated. They developed a number of novel solutions to help them prioritize offers based on point of contact, channel, and customer preference.

To meet deadlines, their initial release worked on an overnight schedule. As such, their predictions were still somewhat hit-and-miss; the models had no way of accommodating customers who had already rejected an offer earlier in the day. In those situations, their system would recommend the same product over and over again, ad infinitum.

Their next project fixed this. Over the next few months they took another step and included real-time information in their recommendations processes. It was at this point where they realized they had the perfect engine to improve other business processes. They'd had a significant impact on sales efficiency. Over drinks one evening, they realized they could have a similar impact on servicing efficiency.

As with most organizations, sales ensure sustainability. They provide the revenue that keeps the company solvent. Servicing, however, is what builds loyalty. Having a good relationship with customers can't guarantee they'll buy another product. What it will do is increase the odds of being at the table the next time the customer has a need. The problem is that servicing is usually expensive. Its returns are long-term, something that doesn't gel well with quarterly targets.

This team realized that they had a massive opportunity. By reusing the predictive real-time multichannel capabilities they'd developed across the sales arm of the business, they'd likely achieve a level of customer relationship unheard of in the industry. That's just what they did.

To explain why this was so significant, put yourself in the shoes of a car enthusiast. You've probably bought at least one expensive car, maybe more. For those people, insurance is a necessary evil. In making the decision about whom to insure with, cost is a key consideration. Most likely, so is ease of claim. The last thing they want is to see their prized asset get damaged.

What the team realized was that they had the perfect engine to both help the customer *and* reduce their own costs. First, they established data feeds from a number of meteorological sites. Then, they created a number of detection routines that cross-referenced damaging weather patterns against geolocated policy holders. By merging the combined data with policy data, they could work out in real time:

- Which customers were likely to see damaging weather such as hail
- When the weather was likely to hit
- Whether the customer had a garage or other protective location they used

A few hours before the weather was due to hit, they'd automatically send out an SMS with a warning and, if appropriate, a personalized suggestion they might want to garage their car. It was automatic, it was cheap, it was personal, and, more important, it was useful.

Through reusing their capabilities across multiple business problems, they helped transform the organization's overall approach to customer engagement. Shortly afterward they extended the same approach to a broad-based outbound campaign to warn people to bring in their washing and the like. And, they kept going.

Common Characteristics

Organizations that exhibit this perspective are driven by the constant need to improve. Their desire for continual efficiency and efficacy gains becomes a deep-rooted belief; they understand both the value of data as well the need to act. Through hard-won experience, they also know how to execute. Their challenge is no longer selling the value. Instead, it's making it pervasive.

Strongly defined processes increasingly become the norm and the use of analytics to support microdecisions becomes the new "business as usual." Entrenched silos increasingly break down, largely because stakeholders across the business can see the value of acting on cross-functional information.

The biggest challenges these organizations face are usually around cultural change. Their leaders understand the importance of continual improvement; it's simply a case of making it stick. While there are usually examples of best practice scattered across the organization, the goal is to make them constantly applied. This is about as hard as one would expect; usually, it involves going directly up against what people are comfortable with.

Some indicators of an organization that's embedded this perspective into their culture include:

- **Considered execution.** Action consistently takes place within the context of broader strategic objectives. Automation of microdecisions becomes the standard operating model. The focus of the organization moves to progressive differentiation rather than short-term tactical advantages.
- **Integrated coordination.** Business units maintain their primary focus on external measures but consistently work together to achieve cross-functional outcomes. Rather than focusing on

sales opportunities, the organization centers itself around *solving the customer's problems*.

- **Incremental value.** Instead of one-off improvements, the dominant culture is one focused on continuous improvement. In parallel, funding is geared toward internal opportunities with higher rates of return.

- **Being the leader.** The dominant culture is one focused on being better than the market. The organization is focused on doing things other competitors would likely find impossible.

- **Improvement targeting.** Performance management is focused on *scale* of outcomes. Reward is geared toward achieving higher-than-average rates of return or efficiency improvements.

- **Beating the benchmark.** Focus shifts from achieving parity to beating parity. Analytically related activities are more advanced in comparison to intelligent peers.

- **Competency-centricity.** Focus shifts from the role to the competencies that drive the role. Teams have well-defined support structures that align management structures to competencies, not technologies or roles. Developing human capital is seen as a core part of the business and the organization excels in developing talent.

- **Reused capability.** The business is consistently reusing existing capabilities to fuel advantage and differentiation. Economies of scale and scope start to emerge.

- **Opportunity-based debate.** Accurate and trusted data has become so pervasive that little if any debate focuses on the problems or facts. Instead, discussion centers around which opportunities the organization should pursue. Disagreement revolves around which opportunities would provide the greatest strategic and tactical benefits.

- **Managed utilities.** Internal support structures are so efficient, cost-effective, and responsive that leveraging and paying for them is no different from turning on a tap and paying the water company for the water consumed. The use of information and analytics is pervasive in all aspects of the business and is treated as a given.

Expanding the Culture

Organizations that have hit this point truly understand the value of business analytics. They've seen the benefits, they know the potential, and like an addict, they crave more. Their focus moves from delivery to transformation; like missionaries, everyone involved in the project starts proselytizing the benefits to anyone who will listen. Their goal is not to just increase the value they're generating. Instead, it's to convert nonbelievers and transform the *entire* organization.

Assuming the organizational is already heavily focused on value creation, it's at this point where it becomes about more than just business analytics. Instead, it becomes about organizational strategy. Expanding the culture further involves a broad organizational commitment to directly compete on data. Not every organization needs to go this far; realistically, most probably don't. There are many sources of competitive differentiation. In the context of broader strategy, business analytics is just another option from many.

There are, however, significant advantages to establishing it as a cornerstone. Digitization will continue to affect every industry sector over upcoming decades. And, coping with the age of uncertainty will require ever-increasingly complex analytical capabilities. *Every* organization benefits from a better ability to analyze the information it has access to.

Anything beyond value creation and continuous improvement requires clear and overt senior executive commitment. It implies a new business model, one centered on information. In some organizations, this is simply a logical step. In others, it's a revolution fueled by an internal visionary. In both cases, it's impossible without the backing of the board, the leadership team, and potentially even the shareholders.

REVOLUTIONARY DISRUPTION

This final perspective is relatively rare. Organizations at this point have established the right culture, management structure, measurement framework, and technology platform to drive sustainable competitive differentiation. For them, business analytics *is* a point of differentiation, no different from customer-centricity or product design. Above all else, they value *disruption*. They become revolutionaries, focused on reinventing their markets.

More important, this approach reflects a philosophy, not a destination. Even though the organization may have seen significant returns, there's nothing to say that they have exhausted every source of business analytics–based value. They've achieved a level of value measurement, automation, and repeatability that allows them to start truly driving economies of scope.

Getting to this point is quite difficult. Globally, there are few organizations that have truly achieved this level of capability at a functional level, let alone at an enterprise level. Those that have tend to be acknowledged as the leaders in their markets. However, because this perspective relies heavily on the broader culture, it's still surprisingly easy for an organization to regress. Just because an organization is truly mature does not mean they have to stay there. As stated earlier, it can take five to seven years to enact real cultural change.[3] This cuts both ways: just as it may take seven years to create a culture, an organization can regress given seven years of inattention or diverted attention. With a typical managerial hire holding the role for roughly three years, that's as brief as two poor managerial hires.

From here, business analytics is a key part of strategic planning. It's not only assumed that new business initiatives will capitalize on business analytics in some way, it's outright expected. Projects that do *not* include business analytics in some way are actively deprioritized in favor of those that do, largely because those that don't have an increased risk of failure. Optimization happens as a matter of course, in terms of both outbound activities as well as internal effort. Inefficiencies are quickly identified and actively managed with the results pushed out across other groups.

While many organizations are at least superficially interested in embracing this perspective, it's not always realistic. Become a disruptor involves reinventing the organization. For an organization that differentiates based on incremental improvements to existing product design, this may simply be a leap too far. And, there's nothing wrong with that; innovation can happen anywhere. Big data and business analytics are simply *another* opportunity for differentiation, not the *only* source.

Industries characterized by large amounts of data will increasingly see this approach as being a preferred source of competitive advantage, largely because it offers so many advantages across the business. Whether it's through a desire to become this type of organization or a need to understand one's competitors, being aware of what this perspective entails is essential.

Common Characteristics

This represents a pinnacle of execution; rather than follow a single model, organizations that have achieved this level redefine it. Some of the biggest indicators of an organization that's adopted this perspective are:

- **Considered optimization.** Activity is continually optimized to maximize return. Competing priorities and opportunities are prioritized automatically. The focus of the organization moves to holistic efficiency and sustained differentiation.

- **Dynamic value.** The dominant culture is one comfortable with cannibalization and continual change. Business units achieve a state of balanced dynamic tension, reinventing as well as improving. Through revolutionary innovation, the organization focuses on solving problems the customers didn't know they had.

- **Being the disruptor.** Business analytics and the use of information are seen as a differentiator by the leadership team. The organization is focused on entering new markets.

- **Differentiation targeting.** Performance management is focused on being best in class. Reward is geared toward achieving excellence.

- **Ignoring the benchmark.** Focus shifts from beating parity to ignoring parity as being meaningless. The organization sets the benchmark and competitors benchmark their competitiveness on the organization in question.

- **Attractive capability.** Focus shifts from competencies to attracting excellence. The quality of competencies and potential for knowledge gain become a magnet for global talent. Being the market leader creates its own draw within the labor market and hiring highly skilled resources becomes increasingly easy.

■ **Market-based debate.** Discussion centers on how best to transform and grow the business. Success through a relentless focus on effective execution is treated as a given. The challenge is seen as maintaining the level of differentiation the organization has achieved.

■ **Democratized empowerment.** Internal support structures start to shrink; rather than requiring centralized support, the ability to analyze, profile, and act on information has become the status quo.

Apart from getting there, the biggest challenge faced by organizations that embrace this perspective is simply maintaining their position long enough to establish a self-sustaining culture. Competitive differentiation is a never-ending process and the organization's philosophy needs to align to this.

NOTES

1. Robert M. Pirsig, *Zen and the Art of Motorcycle Maintenance: An Inquiry into Values* (New York: William Morrow, 1974).
2. James Taylor, *Decision Management Systems: A Practical Guide to Using Business Rules and Predictive Analytics* (Upper Saddle River, NJ: IBM/Pearson, 2012).
3. John P. Kotter, *Leading Change* (Boston: Harvard Business Review, 2012).

CHAPTER 4

The Intelligent Enterprise

Organizations are, by and large, pretty dumb. Shows like *The Office* and comics like *Dilbert* are funny not because they're absurd but because at times they hit a little too close to home. Steering an organization can sometimes seem like a constant fight against chaos—there's political intrigue, competing points of view, and sometimes even an active desire to subvert the system. One of the most stunning cases I've come across involved a business that actually ran an entire shadow IT department. They were eventually caught when they migrated their customer engagement system off their (already deployed) isolated network onto the cloud.

Culture is essential. So is capability. Culture might enable the vision, but without supporting skills, processes, technology, and data there's only good intentions. The goal in making it real is to try to tame the chaos inherent in managing highly complex systems and transform into an intelligent enterprise.

Most organizations are united in a common objective. Despite this, people still act independently. Everyone knows their role but all too frequently people act in isolation. It works, but only to a degree; faced with instability or a changing market, the organization struggles. Quality suffers, cost increases, and inefficiencies abound.

A truly intelligent enterprise operates like our nervous system. It's adaptive, agile, and flexible, able to respond quickly and appropriately

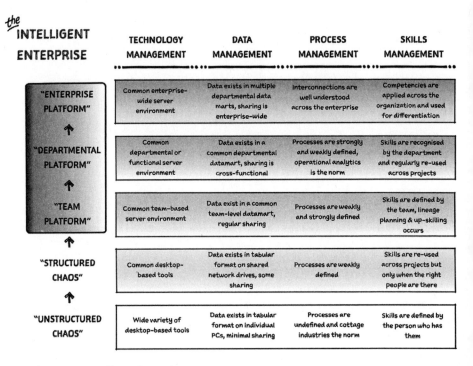

Figure 4.1 Intelligent Enterprise

to external stimuli. Faced with a threat, it mobilizes quickly and takes appropriate action. Interactions are sophisticated and tailored to opportunities and threats. On encountering either, *everything* that's needed is quickly deployed and engaged. Action and response is seamless, instantaneous, and automatic.

This chapter covers the *intelligent enterprise*, as shown in Figure 4.1. The five levels it describes are progressive; they represent the path usually taken by organizations that focus on building capability. Real value starts at level three and continues from there.

LEVEL 1: UNSTRUCTURED CHAOS

Every organization has to start somewhere. Typically, that "somewhere" is rarely where the organization actually *wants* to be. To paraphrase, every beginning starts with darkness and chaos.

Organizations at the lowest level of capability are best described as "confusing." They're characterized by *unstructured chaos*. Everyone is working hard; it's just not always clear how or why they're doing it. Like the proverbial sausage factory, no one really wants to think too hard about what's being used to make the final decision. Because of this, quality is hard to measure. When decisions work, no one wants to know how they were made. When they don't, no one knows why. Because of fragmented processes and data, unpicking the final result is almost impossible.

At this level, people get the job done. However, they also do whatever it takes to get the job done, often leading to highly variable quality and efficiency. Processes are almost consistently ad hoc, bespoke, and usually reactive. Firefighting is more than just a quick fix; it's business as usual. Things succeed not through planning or design but usually through the heroic effort of motivated individuals.

Freedom Can Be Constraining

One of the clearest examples of an organization in this state was one that started with the right foundations but somehow ended up somewhere they really didn't want to be. They started by doing everything right. The interest in business analytics came from the top down. They built the company around information and even went so far as to establish a broadly defined center of excellence. They understood the difference between discovery and operational analytics. Whether through sanity or serendipity, they even managed to solve many of the structural issues that inhibit delivery.

Unfortunately, they got one thing wrong. They gave every data scientist the almost total freedom to select his or her tool of choice. Intuitively, this made sense; it was hoped that it would promote access to best-of-breed capabilities, align tools to existing skills, and make it easy to onboard people by giving them the ability to choose their own working environment. Superficially, the theory was sound.

Unfortunately, practice diverged from theory. Giving people choice also means having to accept that people *will* exercise their right to make choices. What started out as a handful of tools rapidly exploded into a veritable laundry list of every possible tool under the sun, most of which were invisible to their unfortunate IT department.

This was great for the analysts. They had freedom and control. Empowerment is empowering—what's not to like? Strategically though, it led to countless integration and execution issues. Because tools were dependent on the person, it became extremely difficult to create repeatable processes. Filling a role required not only domain knowledge but specific technical and tool knowledge. In the worst cases, some roles were so tightly coupled to individuals that when people were sick, everything would stop. Because no one else knew how to use the missing person's tools, no one else could do his or her job.

Alone, this operational risk was unacceptable. However, their real problems ran deeper. Because everyone was using different tools, modules, and coding standards, it also became extremely difficult to take action on insight. In one case, the discovery team had deep experience in using Python and R. Sadly, no one in the operational team knew how to turn what were largely untested processes into production-grade routines. Even worse, these same data scientists were in high demand. When they eventually left for other opportunities, the intellectual property they had built stagnated and eventually died a grim death because no one else knew how to use it.

After a few years of operating like this, their leadership team knew they had a problem. Unfortunately, the system they had designed had grown so organically and chaotically that they no longer knew how it worked. Every time they tried to make a change their analysts almost revolted. And so they became stuck, trapped in the monster they'd unintentionally created.

Common Characteristics

Organizations do function at this level. They just carry far more cost and operational risk than they need to. They also rarely manage to coalesce their latent capabilities into any real form of differentiation.

Some indicators of an organization operating at this level are:

- **Personal tools.** Analysts use a wide variety of desktop-centric tools with choice largely defined by personal preference.
- **Data-focused effort.** Analysts spend significant amounts of time trying to source, manage, and exchange data between semi-compatible tools.
- **Fragmented data.** Data is fragmented and centered around product, process, or at best, organizational silos.

- **Perpetual reinvention.** Team-members each create their own repository and usually start from scratch every time they have a new project.

- **Undefined processes.** Processes are largely undefined, extremely manual, and require substantial effort to execute.

- **Unaware and overpaid.** Vendor management for analytics tools is limited and largely ineffectual, forcing higher-than-necessary licensing costs.

- **Selfish hoarding.** Analytical data is stored on individuals' personal computers and very little (if any) reuse occurs between analysts.

- **Big-chief syndrome.** Competencies are linked to the individual and skills are a source of job protection.

- **The haystack method.** Competencies are rarely applied across projects in a consistent way and finding value is as difficult as searching for a needle in a haystack.

Taking the Next Step

Getting past this point requires acknowledging that sometimes structure is necessary. Somewhat counterintuitively, it's about limiting choice, reducing flexibility, and improving repeatability.

Flexibility encourages innovation and agility. However, too much of a good thing can hurt. Without a way to commercialize good ideas, all the benefits of innovation are lost. Organizations operate in a different context from individuals. What may work brilliantly for one person rarely scales to a larger system without some deliberate design and planning.

The starting point is usually to start profiling current activities across people, process, data, and technology. Are there too many tools? Conduct an audit and start rationalizing them. Are there undefined processes? Understand what people do and what outputs their customers are expecting. Are there PC-based data structures? Consolidate them onto a shared environment. Is there limited reuse of skills across projects? Profile existing skills and start thinking about capabilities rather than individuals.

The objective at this level is simply to create some structure, even if it's limited in the first instance. More than anything else, it's about exposing current practices and simply *understanding* them. Trying to *fix* things is often a step too soon and too far in these cases. Without knowing where the problems are, where attention is being focused, or even how effectively people are doing their jobs, every "fix" carries the risk of making things worse.

LEVEL 2: STRUCTURED CHAOS

Chaotic systems aren't necessarily random. That might sound strange, but consider a Lorenz attractor. Within a truly chaotic system, it's impossible to predict the position of any element at any particular point in time. That doesn't mean that the system itself doesn't follow higher-order patterns. When this happens, one has hit a point of *structured chaos*. While individual elements might still behave randomly, their overall behaviors might just be random around a broader pattern.

Organizations at this point have started to tame the chaos. Rather than try to force structure, they take a softer approach, balancing local choice with global requirements. They set constraints, establish an intended functional or divisional strategy, and try to get the entirety of the organization to comply with it. As is probably unsurprising, this is where most organizations sit. Standards are meaningless if they're not complied with; the true test as to whether an organization is at this level or the next is real-world compliance with guidelines and strategy. Having a standard operating environment is one thing. Having the business *comply* with that standard operating environment is another.

The biggest barrier to success at this point is unconscious ignorance. These organizations are usually sophisticated enough to know that information is valuable. They've taken the first steps toward turning what's usually an ad hoc, undefined activity into a core, if still somewhat basic, competency. However, their lack of awareness of what's possible and what "good" looks like inhibits their ability to scale or create tangible value. Often, their belief that they've solved the problem by defining a governance model is a major inhibitor. They become self-deluded and convince themselves that they've succeeded without taking the time to check whether their strategy and intent is actually happening.

Total Agility Can Be Costly

A prime example of this type of organization discovered this almost unintentionally. As an outsider looking in, they appeared to be a real leader in their sector. They deeply understood the value of information. Almost to the last, their analysts were extremely capable and intelligent. They had rationalized their analytics tools, they had an internal structure which made it easy to engage with data scientists, and their key performance indicators were cleanly aligned with tactical and strategic objectives.

Despite this, they had some rather strange quirks. For one, they lacked a central processing or data storage environment. To most of their leadership team, this wasn't seen as a problem. They simply bought big PCs and lots of local storage. In practice, they even sometimes held this up as an example of their ingenuity and innovation; by taking the road less traveled, they felt they had created a highly innovative, flexible, and agile business.

Another was their apparent lack of structure. Where most of their competitors were struggling with overly defined governance models, they had highly flexible support and delivery frameworks. More than just "getting" agile methods, they practically lived them. This was again held up as a prime example of their ability to innovate. However, while the milestones they had to work through were always clear, what wasn't was how they'd generate insight or act on it. Everyone did things differently.

For a long time, everything seemed to hum like a well-oiled machine. Unfortunately, one year they experienced a perfect storm of three things that shook the status quo.

The first of these was the resignation of one of their most senior analysts. The talent loss was bad enough. Unfortunately, he was also the developer of their core customer insight engine. During his handover, it became frighteningly apparent that no matter how much he tried to bring others up to speed, no one else had any hope of understanding how his application worked in the time he had left. This lack of process suddenly created a massive operational risk.

It also led to the second event. Shortly after he left, the application stopped working. This in itself wasn't too surprising; despite their best efforts, they hadn't been able to maintain it. Unfortunately, they also found out that when the insight engine went down, so did their customer relationship management (CRM) system. Unknown to the team maintaining it, the insight engine had been feeding target lists to the CRM system every night. When the lists stopped coming, the CRM system produced an exception and halted *all* outbound marketing. The theoretical operational risk had just become actual losses.

The final blow was the complete and total loss of critical pricing data. A well-meaning but misguided junior analyst ran out of space on the network drive while doing some data mining. Knowing that the senior analyst was no longer employed by the organization, he thought it made sense to delete that analyst's folder. Unfortunately, the directories he deleted contained both archived as well as active data—active data that was still a direct input to a variety of other processes. When those directories disappeared, a number of pricing models stopped updating correctly. Even worse, these errors were subtle enough that they weren't identified for weeks afterward. While the final costs were never calculated, everyone knew they'd lost customers.

These losses in quick succession forced the executive leadership team to start asking questions. In a few short months, they'd lost money, talent, customers, and reputation. That same flexibility that had been such a strength had suddenly become a major liability.

Thankfully, they were self-aware enough to know not to replace everything wholesale. Their flexibility and agility *had* created a source of competitive advantage. Rather than getting rid of it, they rightly realized that they should instead *augment* it with structure in the right places. Shortly afterward they launched a transformation project to:

- Improve governance and structure for the operational use of analytics.
- Establish a focused model for human capital development and intellectual property retention.
- Identify and replicate best practices in operational processes through process management.
- Centralize information assets and ensure appropriate security/ privacy controls were in place.
- Establish a centralized computational platform that could support mission-critical uses of analytics.

Much to their surprise, what started as an attempt to mitigate operational risk actually turned into a source of significant value. Their efficiency levels increased. So did their ability to embed analytics into decision making. Their attention to culture and talent retention became a draw card for talent in its own right. And, the centralization of their information and analytics tools helped reduce their operating costs.

Common Characteristics

Organizations at this point "don't know what they don't know." They know analytics is important but their use is inconsistent. While it's not always the case, they're often guided by people who are familiar with using analytics mainly for research. They usually appreciate the need for a team approach.

More than anything else, they focus on insight. To their credit, they understand the importance of analytics. They try to encourage the use of common tools. And, they encourage data sharing. However, they rarely understand an extremely important concept: operational analytics.

Business analytics is more than just insight. Data science and exploratory analysis is important. Without action, however, all that insight is worthless. The most efficient way to act on insight is to embed those same analytics into operational processes. Improving one decision might add a little value. Improving *hundreds* of microdecisions can create tremendous value.[1] Of all possible applications, the use of operational analytics offers one of the greatest returns on investment.[2]

Organizations at this level are still fundamentally person-centric in their technology, process, and data design. While in principle they encourage sharing, their architecture is such that they simply *cannot* automate their analytical processes. And because of this, they inevitably constantly struggle to change their analysis from a collection of bespoke approaches into enterprise-grade processes.

Some indicators of an organization operating at this level are:

- **Team tools.** While analysts select their analytics tools from a predefined list or standard operating environment, these tools are still predominantly desktop-centric.
- **Search-focused effort.** Analysts spend most of their time trying to *find* data rather than recreate it.

- **Decentralized data.** Data is still centered on organizational silos but cross-referenced points are defined and understood.
- **Avoidable reinvention.** Team members share their data in common storage areas, even if reuse is still often low in practice.
- **Weakly defined processes.** Processes exist but are undefined outside inputs and outputs. When someone leaves, his or her replacement reinvents everything else from scratch.
- **Aware but uncertain.** Vendor management becomes aware of overpayment but is uncertain about what is necessary and what is sufficient.
- **Well-intentioned chaos.** Analytical data is stored on shared drives because of a belief in the value of information reuse. Unfortunately, little reuse happens in practice largely because of the complexity involved in trying to track down information.
- **Polymath syndrome.** While competencies are identified and applied across projects, the success of a project depends largely on who's working on it.
- **The cargo cult.** The path to value is based on subjective experience, and competencies, tools, and processes are selected based on what worked last time, not necessarily what makes the most sense.

Taking the Next Step

Getting past this point requires the commitment to start reengineering the way the organization works. It involves asking fundamental questions about why things are designed the way they are across people, process, data, and technology. In many cases, this is linked to a broader "lean design" or "transformation" initiative, tasked with making things simpler, more agile, and more efficient.

It's usually at this point where many organizations start to balk at the implications of becoming smarter in their operational decision making, largely because they start to appreciate the sheer scale of the challenge. At the extreme, it involves deconstructing every processes, one by one, and mercilessly hunting down and eliminating *every* non-value-added activity. The goal is to decouple the analytics from the individual, thereby turning it into a team competency. This is rarely easy; inevitably, it involves slaughtering more than a few sacred cows.

When starting out, most organizations find it difficult to do *any* analytics. Because the starting benchmark is so low, simply getting to the point of using analytics within a handful of operational processes is often enough to drive a surprising amount of value. This pales in comparison to the value offered through automated and operational analytics; rather than augmenting five or six decision-making activities, it becomes possible to have an impact on hundreds or even thousands.

Getting to this point means things need to change. And, making these changes happen is challenging. Of all capability improvements, this is arguably the hardest. People need to work differently, and behaviors need to shift from being "cowboy analysts" to team players. Making this leap is difficult. However, the benefits of doing so are significant.

While still a step short of transformation or differentiation, the major benefit of making these changes is operating efficiency and cost management. Consolidating technology increases purchasing leverage with a smaller set of vendors. With focus, this reduces vendor management and systems administration and maintenance costs.

These benefits also extend to developing people. By identifying and nurturing desired and valuable skills, organizations reduce the cost of hiring and retaining resources. Creating strongly defined processes also allows organizations to start automating non-value-added activities. This improves efficiency and often creates the opportunity to create a leaner, more agile organization.

The core objective at this level is to make things more efficient. More than anything else, it's about reengineering current practices to embody the basics of leading practice. The big step is moving beyond *understanding* what's wrong and actually *fixing* it. It's at this level where change management becomes the single most important factor in success. Without actually getting people to work differently, unlimited technology investment will nonetheless inevitably lead to "business as usual."

LEVELS 3–5: THE INTELLIGENT ENTERPRISE

Fixing things is excellent. Unfortunately, it's still not enough for organizations interested in repeatable innovation. The gap between "things working" and "best practice" is a broad one. Closing it requires achieving a certain minimum level of capability. They've become the *intelligent enterprise*.

Organizations at this level recognize that business analytics is a journey, not a destination. While their use might not be truly enterprise-wide, their platform architecture is such that they *could* eventually replicate those same capabilities across the organization if they needed to.

They have achieved a level of process-centricity, moving away from artisanal applications to mass-production methods. While there's a large gap between a single example of best practice and consistent use across the entire organization, they understand that there are benefits to replicating automated methods. Most important, they take constant steps toward best practice, slowly making it pervasive across as many business processes as they can.

Common Characteristics

Process automation and the use of operational analytics becomes, if not the norm, at least relatively common. Some of the biggest indicators of organizations at this point are:

- **Common tools.** Analytical tools are standardized at least within teams, usually across a department, and sometimes across the entire organization. They are predominantly server-centric with desktop-based tools being used almost exclusively to support niche R&D applications or to fill gaps where it would be uneconomical to deploy server-centric tools.

- **Leverage-focused effort.** Analysts spend most of their time trying to reuse data and assets rather than recreate existing assets.

- **Centralized data.** Analysts and data scientists share their analytical and value-added data in centralized repositories, whether they be appliances, traditional warehouses, distributed file systems like Hadoop, or NoSQL repositories like mongoDB.

- **Deliberate reuse.** Team members share their data in centralized marts and activity is centered around reusing what's already there.

- **Strongly defined processes.** Processes are strongly defined where they need to be integrated with operational activities.

- **Aware and certain.** Vendor management becomes aware of overpayment and links investment to broader capability and value creation.

- **Optimistic sharing.** Analytical data is stored in common server-based environments and reuse happens functionally, departmentally, or even on an enterprise-wide scale.

- **The efficient machine.** Reuse of skills decouples project success from team participation. Projects succeed because of access to capability, not access to specific individuals.

- **The empire.** Competencies are explicitly recognized within the context of a formalized human capital development model.

Taking the Next Step

In many ways, there is no "moving past this point." Organizations that have built a platform to guide decision making no longer look for a finite series of point solutions. Instead, they appreciate that there are an infinite number of possible improvements that can be made. Their point of view shifts from one of "fix this, fix that" to one of continuous improvement where best practices are identified, nurtured, and replicated across the entire organization. They reuse their capabilities across people, process, data, and technology to drive maximum value. Their platform use progressively moves through "embedding" into "differentiating."

Getting to this point starts only from one of two locations. The *organic path* begins when a particular group within the organization is placed under such severe tension that they need to actively search for a new approach. Without this tension, "business as usual" remains the norm. As they develop their capabilities, they build a microculture within the organization that, if sustained for long enough, is eventually recognized by parties inside and outside the organization. Other groups learn from their successes and, given sufficient leadership and motivation for change, their culture ends up being replicated by other groups. Over a long enough period of time, this self-replicating culture ends up becoming pervasive.

This large-scale transformation through organic replication seems relatively rare. More frequently this cultural transformation halts either with the group in question or, in some cases, with the group they're part of. Without a clear commitment from the leadership team to sustain and replicate their positive culture, their approach frequently only exists for as long as the people driving the cultural change keep working for the organization. Given the high demand both internally and externally for people capable of creating value from big data and business analytics, their employment is typically far shorter than the time it takes to create a self-sustaining culture.

The *directed path* starts from the top and flows from there. Either through external tension or the unique opportunity to create a culture from scratch during the startup phase, the executive leadership team acknowledges the need for a particular culture and makes an explicit decision to create it. Due largely to the public nature of this approach, there are some well-known examples that highlight the impact it can have. Jack "Neutron" Welch reinvented General Electric and grew its revenues from $26 billion to more than $130 billion between 1981 and 2000. Despite starting as a monoline credit agency, Capital One pioneered a strongly data-driven decision-making culture, growing from a spunky startup to a Fortune 500 company.

It's important to remember that examples like this are rare. For every success, there are many examples of stalled or outright failed attempts. Changing an organization's culture is not for the faint of heart; it requires tremendous executive commitment and carries great risk. Change inevitably leads to discomfort and too much discomfort can lead to the loss of positive as well as negative patterns. At some stage the organic approach needs turn into a more direct approach, linking example with executive commitment.

From this point on, the goal is true differentiation. At the lower levels, organizations are usually playing catch-up with their competitors, simply trying to replicate what others have already achieved. From this point on, the organization has achieved a sufficient level of capability and intelligence to become unique. Rather than copying, they invent. Rather than repurpose, they create. And rather than start by looking externally for inspiration, they often start by looking internally; given enough competency, they recognize that their abilities surpass many of the examples that others provide. Equally though, they are self-aware enough to know that the boundaries are constantly expanding. As such they need to stay across leading practices both within and outside their particular industry sector.

This journey is a never-ending one. There are more opportunities for reinvention than there are hours in the day. Rather than being seen as an aspirational goal, *every* organization needs to achieve this level of capability at some point if it is to remain sustainable. In a world where big data is the norm and data offers a core competitive advantage, achieving this level of cultural focus and technical capability isn't optional; it's mandatory. This does not necessarily imply high investment costs. Whether it's through leveraging low-cost, cloud-based commodity infrastructure or through highly differentiated R&D development, the era of pure experience-based competition is over. Rejecting the power of data in a digital world and refusing to mature will inevitably lead to irrelevance.

NOTES

1. James Taylor, *Decision Management Systems: A Practical Guide to Using Business Rules and Predictive Analytics* (Upper Saddle River, NJ: IBM/Pearson, 2012).
2. Evan Stubbs, *Delivering Business Analytics: Practical Guidelines for Best Practice* (Hoboken, NJ: John Wiley & Sons, 2013).

PART
THREE

Making It Real

Culture is essential. So is capability. Creating or reinventing an organization is fraught with risk. Rather than guess, it's always better to take advantage of other people's mistakes and build on the fundamentals. While we'll cover it in more detail in Chapter 8, innovation is actually conceptually easy. There's an idea, there's a plan, and there's action. Getting the design right means making sure that the structure and operating model fit within that framework.

Having said that, no plan leaves the battlefield unscathed. It is possible, however, to increase the odds of success as long as *you know what you're trying to achieve*. Few examples demonstrate the importance of continual self-assessment better than that of James.*

James came from a background in economics. His ability to blend theory with practice led to rapid advancement, quickly moving from driving tactical efficiencies in customer contact management to owning the organization's customer strategy.

---

*James represents an amalgam of a wide variety of case studies based on very real people and their experiences. Lest readers look for themselves, he's a blend of a variety of people who took a similar journey.

Reporting directly to the chief marketing officer, James had been put in charge of:

- Increasing products per customer
- Improving margin
- Raising customer satisfaction (measured through Net Promoter Score)

Like many leaders, James looked internally *and* externally for inspiration. Internally, James found that his organization was severely underutilizing their data assets. While there was no shortage of people with great ideas, few of those ideas made it into practice. In many ways, James was lucky; while creativity wasn't a core part of his organization's culture, he still managed to find more than enough people who were willing to support a new way of working.

Externally, James found validation; big data and big data analytics were clearly the flavor of the month, if not the decade. Whether he talked to competitors, partners, vendors, or analysts, the importance of information in driving outcomes was the dominant message. The only question was, what was he going to do about it?

James outlined a three-point plan. First, he'd establish a pure-play data science team to generate insights. Then, he'd use that team to improve business results. Finally, he'd extend the scope of his team to diversify his organization's business model through ancillary services.

The plan seemed solid. His logic was strong and James quickly garnered the support of the chief marketing officer and the chief financial officer. Unfortunately, James didn't quite get the money he was looking for. While he had asked for a team of eight, he had been given authority to hire a team of four. While he had asked for a significant technology investment to build a new platform, he'd been given a small discretionary budget.

Despite this, his targets didn't change. His leadership team agreed with his vision. They just didn't feel confident enough to give him what he wanted. He'd asked for a mandate and money; he'd been given one of the two.

Things went badly from day one. As he expected, there was plenty of data available. As also expected, most of it was unstructured, incomplete, and usually inconsistent. For example, an early scan found eight different ways of counting customers, all of which were technically correct but totally different. Depending on whether one defined a customer as a billing address, an account, or a person, the variance could be as high as 20 percent. While James knew in advance that getting the data ready was going to be a challenge, he still underestimated how difficult it would actually be.

Unfortunately, this proved to be the least of his worries. After spending a number of months simply trying to get the basics working, James hit an unexpected roadblock. After much blood, sweat, and tears, his team found some insights of critical value. Traditionally, the organization had always viewed customers within segments as substitutable. While every customer was important, one "young professional" was seen as the same as any other.

On top of this segment-based customer view, James's team overlaid current and long-term profitability. As expected, some segments were more profitable than others. This matched stage of life and wealth; richer customers at the peak of their earning capacity tended to spend more.

When profitability was taken into account, some of these segments split cleanly into two new sub-segments. Within these groups, up to 80 percent of customers were either breakeven or loss-making when servicing and retention costs were taken into account. The remainder was wildly profitable and contributed to almost 70 percent of the company's operating profit.

This wasn't new; marketing and sales had been struggling with this for almost a year. Even though groups of people showed common behaviors, their spending and products per person varied significantly within those groups. So, while their segmentation model was useful in *describing* their customers, it didn't always help improve their marketing return on investment.

What *was* new was what James found when he included customer satisfaction. Based on current value alone, there was no obvious relationship between satisfaction and profitability. In some situations, strong promoters were actually unprofitable. In others, detractors were highly profitable.

This seemed counterintuitive. However, things made sense when future value was included. Even though satisfaction had little to do with current profitability, it had a *significant* impact on future profitability. While not the only factor in determining customer value, James found that promoters in specific segments would consistently acquire more products per customer over a three-year period. This in turn led to higher profitability.

The answer was clear. Rather than just servicing already profitable customers, the organization needed to include supportive but not-yet-profitable customers from specific segments. The combination of behavioral analysis, life-stage marketing, and net promoter score could give them a level of relevancy that none of them in isolation could match. By adjusting their servicing and retention strategy, they could have a significant impact on aggregate customer profitability while also reducing servicing costs.

It was a great solution. Unfortunately, James struggled to get the rest of the organization on board with his approach. As he found out, simply having the backing of his leadership team wasn't enough. Without it, he would have never received enough authority to even have a discussion about his team's discoveries. Even with it, there was no guarantee that anyone would care. What should have taken weeks to move into production ended up taking months with most of James's time spent convincing people that this was the right thing to do.

By the end of the year, James had managed to demonstrate a reduction in marketing spend with no impact on cancellations or customer satisfaction. He also had the vocal backing of their vice president for customer engagement and experience. And, he had strong expectations that the changes they'd made to their servicing strategy would see them generating compound returns over the next two years.

Unfortunately, his end-of-year review didn't quite go as he'd expected. While the leadership team were congratulatory, they were also clear that he'd failed to achieve his objectives. He *had* demonstrated that business analytics would and did add value to the business. However, he had also fallen short of his original projections. The meeting ended on a rather bittersweet note. They agreed to invest more into his group over the upcoming year. They also flagged that he'd underperformed and that they expected better performance the following year.

When he looked back, he realized he'd made two simple mistakes. First, he'd taken on an impossible mission. In retrospect, his original

estimated investment was right. Rather than accepting a token investment, he should have argued for either reduced scope or his actual
requirements. While it might have led to an uncomfortable discussion, it
would have been better to demonstrate clear rather than clouded success.

Second, he had grossly underestimated the importance of culture
and change management in delivering value. He'd devoted almost
half the year to convincing people that the new approach was better
than the old, time he hadn't factored into his plans. While there was
no getting around the need for persuasion, he'd initially wasted time
thinking that the evidence alone would be enough. It was only after
he'd realized that weeks were slowly passing with no change that he'd
adjusted his strategy.

However, it wasn't all bad news. He'd achieved the most important thing of all—a measurable impact on the business. Instead of simply generating insight, he'd managed to get the organization to act on
that insight to create value. Without this, it's questionable whether his
group would have lasted another year.

When he planned his next year's strategy, he built it around three
principles: realistic pragmatism, change management, and value creation.

The next three years were different. He consistently exceeded his
targets and removed all doubt about the importance of customer loyalty in current and future profitability. He expanded his organization's
use of loyalty information through all inbound and outbound channels. And, he transformed the way his organization used information
in customer interactions.

James did a lot of things right. He also discovered that it's harder
than one might suppose. His eventual success came from setting his
group up correctly, making sure they were focused on the right things,
and getting the right people. That's what this part focuses on.

Much like building a house, it lays the foundations on which the
final part builds a model that enables innovation. Also like building
a house, there's no such thing as a single "right" architecture. Some
people like open plans; others like Californian bungalows. What's right
for someone comes down to what they need and what they want, not
what other people think is best. Not everyone needs a mansion.

Every organization is different. It would be insane to suggest that
every organization should follow exactly the same design. Exactly like

building a house though, there are building codes that should be followed. Contrary to some local councils or homeowners associations, they're not there to constrain or irritate. They're there to make sure things don't unexpectedly fail.

This part provides those codes. It focuses on three areas:

1. Organizational design
2. Operating models
3. Human capital

Chapter 5 reviews how organizations can structure their teams and manage the associated costs. It covers various interaction models and describes common services these groups normally offer.

Chapter 6 defines the types of value these groups need to create. It provides an operating model that explains the major activities that need to take place. This model acts as a way of dividing responsibilities between groups (such as IT and the analytics group) within an organization.

Finally, Chapter 7 outlines a human capital model that can be used to assess, develop, and retain staff. It flags one of the biggest "unknown unknowns" most organizations eventually discover. It also covers the breadth of capabilities and role types organizations need to develop. It highlights why it's almost impossible to find the "right" person and why organizations need to develop teams.

CHAPTER 5

Organizational Design

I t's one thing to know you need something. Knowing where it should go is something else. Not to understate how hard it is to change culture, there's obviously more to success than just setting the right direction. Flourishing through the age of uncertainty requires an *excellent* ability to analyze, predict, and act.

The worst thing to do is to run out and hire people just because someone thinks there's a gap. Instead, the focus should be on making the existing people successful by giving them the right support. They need the right structure, the right focus, and a management mandate to make things happen.

Getting the design right helps tremendously. When correct, it creates economies of scope and scale. These enable structural cost advantages that in some cases can actually create differentiation in their own right. In reinventing an organization, there are four things that should be considered:

1. What should it look like?

2. What should it focus on?

3. What services can it offer?

4. What data does it need?

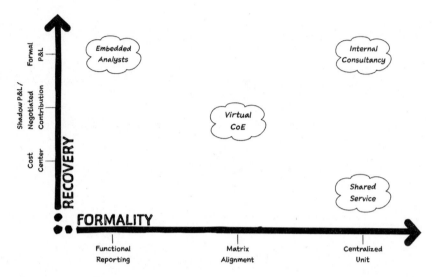

Figure 5.1 Structural Choices

This chapter will answer these questions and lay the foundation for effective organizational design.

WHAT SHOULD IT LOOK LIKE?

Every organization carries baggage. While there's sometimes the unique opportunity to build things from scratch, more often we need to work with what's already there. Getting things right means understanding *where we are* as well as working out where we *should* be. Because of this, moving from generating insight to creating value from big data usually requires change.

At its simplest (and least intrusive), this may involve splitting an existing team into two. One group might focus on change and transformation, the other on generating insight. At the other end of the spectrum lie organizations that totally reinvent themselves around using big data and business analytics as a competitive differentiator.

Sometimes, small steps make a lot of sense. Other times, realizing a big vision requires a big step. When resources are scattered across the organization, structural change can be daunting. Luckily, there's an easy way to consider the benefits and disadvantages of various models. Every group needs a manager, and every group needs to cover its costs somehow. Through these, the major options are presented in Figure 5.1.

Group Formality

The least intrusive method is functional reporting. Analysts are embedded within business units. Often, they're not even formally recognized; they're just the person who knows how to code in Excel. There *are* advantages to this model. For one, it gives business units freedom to invest in the areas they think will provide the greatest value. Unfortunately, it also increases costs in the long run. If and when multiple business units decide that they need access to similar skills, they usually end up hiring similar people. Local efficiencies, while flexible, rarely lead to global efficiencies.

The midway point involves establishing a virtual group. Usually, this has people report to multiple groups through matrix management. Moving everybody into one group is seen as a step too far, too soon. Instead, analysts report to two masters. Analytical resources and headcount continue to reside in functional lines of business (such as marketing or fraud). These business lines manage the analysts' day-to-day workload.

The organization also maintains a secondary line of reporting through to a centralized group, responsible for strategic direction. Rather than internalizing all analytical activities, this centralized group instead focuses its much smaller headcount on aspects usually overlooked by functional lines of business, often including:

- Establishing a common enterprise value measurement framework
- Defining and delivering on an enterprise analytical architecture
- Evangelizing analytics across the organization
- Supporting change management and organizational enablement

This model offers some good advantages. For one, it creates relatively minimal disruption. Additionally, it fills out the organization's capabilities by investing in areas functional units are unlikely to care about. Enterprise transformation, if successful, is valuable. However, it's a rare business unit that's happy to pay for group benefits.

The model does come with disadvantages. The complexity of managing such a model is nontrivial. Resource contention often becomes a major issue when group and functional demands conflict. Directing investment is also challenging; in practice, the centralized group often ends up acting as a diplomat or negotiator, trying to persuade lines of business to "get along" and invest in the right areas.

The most structured model involves establishing a centralized group. The biggest advantage of this model is that without it, it's almost impossible to achieve real economies of scale or scope. This applies to many functions; it can include areas as diverse as:

- Data science and experimentation
- Analytical data management
- Advanced analytics and predictive modelling
- Quality control
- Optimization
- Business intelligence and dashboarding
- Insight operationalization

Of course, this comes at a cost. Scale creates bureaucracy. It also needs an owner, someone who's willing to make sure the group's creating value. An underleveraged group is just more cost and in most cases has a limited life.

A prime example is an analytical center of excellence, covered in greater detail later in this chapter. Often headed up by a chief analytics officer or chief data scientist, it usually exists as a separate functional line of business in its own right. These centers may report directly to the CEO or fall within another line of business with a focus on shared services such as IT. Usually, they're created to pull all analytical resources into one group, tasked with supporting the business. The group maintains its own headcount, budget, and cost center or, more ideally, profit-and-loss statement (real or shadow).

Each approach offers different advantages and drawbacks; none of them is better than any other. For example, establishing a formal model often requires major organizational change and investment.

This formality comes with benefits. For one, it's easier for the rest of the organization to engage with the centralized group. The virtual model requires significantly less investment and preserves existing powerbases. It does, however, increase management complexity and can make engagement challenging. The functional model allows flexibility but prevents scale.

Usually, the right model is dictated by management commitment to business analytics and organizational politics. For many organizations, the virtual model is simply a steppingstone to drive cultural change. For some, the virtual model doesn't go far enough; nothing less than true centralization will do. As will be covered in Chapter 8, the real answer often involves *multiple* models.

Cost Recovery

The second consideration is how analysts cover their costs. One approach is to act as a shared service. Resources are offered "free of charge." In this model a board, leadership team, or other governance committee manages activities and investment. Ideally, this oversight group focuses on value. They prioritize effort based on quantitative and value-based considerations such as strategic objectives or the quantum of return expected.

This is the easiest model to adopt. Given that the teams responsible for generating answers rarely own the outcomes, it's financially hard to measure these groups' profitability. Unfortunately, it also frequently discourages long-term investment; because the group isn't linked to revenue or profit, it's seen as a cost center. Without significant cultural commitment the broader organization is usually reluctant to invest.

An alternative model is to operate using a shadow profit-and-loss statement. Usually, this is based on negotiation and is approved by other lines of business. While not necessarily appearing in the general ledger, the group has a management mandate to demonstrate return on investment. Costs are registered but successes are credited against the group through a shadow tracking system. By doing this, the group can still demonstrate financial outcomes and success despite not having direct control or ownership over revenue streams. Admittedly, there's a heavy emphasis on negotiation and the perpetual temptation to game the system. However, this midpoint at least allows the leadership to track the value of business analytics.

The most sophisticated approach is to establish a formal profit-and-loss statement. Under this model the group is charged with demonstrating internal profitability. Rather than offering services for free, the group uses group allocations or internal resource request-based pricing to charge out its time to other business units. Key performance indicators are often defined as a blended model, balancing total return on investment against maintaining an agreed realization level.

Tactically, the group needs to remain solvent. Strategically, the group needs to be able to demonstrate how its actions have delivered economic returns. In many ways, this model requires the group to act as a chargeable internal consultancy, actively seeking out business and needing to demonstrate return on investment.

This model is a challenging one. The biggest advantage it offers is direct accountability. Unfortunately, it also drives profit-maximizing behaviors. Leaders of the group will naturally chase their biggest customers, neglecting areas of the business that aren't interesting. While it often ensures cost neutrality, in the absence of a broader cultural commitment it rarely leads to organizational transformation.

Each approach offers different advantages and disadvantages. The biggest advantage of the shared service center approach is ease of engagement. Because resources are free and activities are prioritized through a well-defined process, business units have fewer barriers to trying to leverage business analytics. Equally, though, this often increases the complexity of demonstrating return on investment from business analytics. At its worst, demonstrating success becomes a lobbying process. The business analytics team spends the majority of their time convincing other business units to publicly support the business analytics group regardless of outcome.

Running a separate profit-and-loss statement limits this bad behavior. Return on resources is easily demonstrable based on utilization and project success. However, this upfront cost can act as a significant barrier to business unit experimentation, especially in climates of constrained budgets. When budgets are tight, most business units will resist having to pay to do things differently. If this approach isn't supported by a corresponding culture, the group runs a very real risk of self-optimizing and only working with those business units that are most willing to pay, undermining the whole point of an enterprise approach to business analytics.

WHAT SHOULD IT FOCUS ON?

Embedding analysts in business units is a valid option. For one, it's easy—it doesn't require any broader strategy. Just hire the person and set her to work.

Unfortunately, it does little to help with the trends discussed in Chapter 2. While it does allow a great deal of flexibility, it does little to encourage reuse, human capital development, or economies of scale and scope. Left alone without management support or a mandate to work otherwise, people will normally work independently.

The rise of rōnin will eventually force most organizations to think about trying to centralize and reuse their analytical capabilities. Technology is infinitely reproducible; people are not. That's not to say that embedded analysts are a bad thing. As a hiring model, it's an excellent augmentation to centralized approaches. There just aren't enough analysts in the market to realize every opportunity through continually hiring new people.

The decision to set up a central group (in some form) is a logical conclusion. It does, however, inevitably lead to the question of what it should focus on. Every group needs a purpose.

It's helpful to consider a shared group's function along three lines: (1) They can help build knowledge; (2) they can help deliver; or (3) they can help transform the organization. Organizations that decide to centralize their capabilities often call the result Communities of Practice, Competency Centers, or Centers of Excellence.

It's important to recognize that these definitions aren't absolute; you say tom*a*to, I say tom*ah*to. Definitions vary and, as yet, standard names do not exist. They're used here to highlight how structure and focus can vary even when there's a defined departmental or enterprise-wide capability.

Communities of Practice

The lowest-touch model is a community of practice. Communities of practice tend to focus on helping practitioners share and learn from each other. Right or wrong, they're usually the starting point for a leadership team that has realized the value of business analytics but is concerned with making structural changes.

Their primary objective is to nurture skills. They try to cross-pollinate knowledge between those who would, in the absence of the community of practice, rarely cross paths. They do this through regular meetings or conferences. Their focus is to try to get people to network and to share their experience.

Their main attraction is their low-impact nature; they require no structural change whatsoever. It's usually more like a shared club where attendance is encouraged but optional. They develop social capital and promote collaboration.

At best, this is only a halfway house. Their biggest weakness is that they rarely drive any behavioral changes. Awareness is one thing, change another. More often than not, people revert to their comfort zone after attending the get-togethers. This isn't because of a lack of enthusiasm or a resistance to change. It's simply because it's easier to keep doing what one is doing. Many change agents often overlook this limitation and assume that because all the right people have been brought together, change is inevitable.

Despite being a somewhat halfhearted approach, communities of practice still have their benefits. In the absence of anything else, they help to develop awareness of the importance of business analytics. While they tend to be focused on specific applications such as risk, marketing analytics, or business intelligence, they help by mitigating one of the biggest constraints in any large organization—functional separation. Because of this, the function of a community of practice is often eventually blended into a more structured model such as a competency center.

Competency Centers

Competency centers go further. They change the structure of the organization, drawing similar resources into one group. Their model is usually to act as a shared service center to support the broader organization.

Their main attraction is consolidation and enabling economies of scale. Unlike "insights teams," these centers have a narrow focus, usually defined functionally. They may specialize in predictive modeling. They often specialize in business intelligence. They may focus on machine learning. Integral to this focus is a longer-term strategy that outlines how the group will move toward best practice. They often go beyond ad hoc support to include actual delivery. While they don't own the outcome, they'll usually be responsible for making sure their work makes it into production.

There are significant advantages to this model. By drawing common skills into one group, the organization starts developing economies of scale through specialization. Clarity of focus also helps other groups get engaged. When skills are scattered, it's often hard for people to take advantage of latent capabilities. It's far easier for other groups to get engaged when there's a single team to contact.

It's also a tangible demonstration of strategic intent. Creating a defined group does wonders to clarify what the enterprise sees as a potential competitive advantage. It gives the organization a hook to latch onto and experiment with. Even if others don't necessarily understand the domain, they at least know it's there for them to take advantage of.

Despite their advantages, competency centers are still limited. For one, they maintain a siloed delivery approach. Because of their functionally defined focus, their engagement tends to align with traditional business applications and ignores developing enterprise-wide competencies.

For example, a risk competency center has the potential to add tremendous value across the business. In addition to traditional scoring and simulation activities, they could add real value through driving risk-based pricing and augmenting financial planning to incorporate boundary testing. Unfortunately, this rarely happens. In the absence of specific direction, the team will usually gravitate toward traditional risk management processes such as managing operational risk or identifying behavioral or application risk. When one's goal is being utilized rather than driving change, it's easier to sell to current rather than potential customers. Because of this, much of the cross-functional potential of business analytics is lost.

Another disadvantage is that because their domain is taken as a given, the team usually pays little attention to evangelism. A mandate is both a blessing and curse. On one hand, it establishes responsibility. On the other, it's easy to assume that the rest of the organization will be just as interested and supportive.

In practice, this is rarely the case. By definition, any sophisticated area of expertise is niche. Not everyone in the organization will understand it, let alone value it. Business analytics is fundamentally about change and driving change requires proactivity. While it's not inevitable, competency centers often overlook the importance of evangelism and sales. Instead, they fill the role of a pure shared service center, responding to work requests as they file in. They end up being great at supporting business as usual and "known unknowns," but transformation and tackling the "unknown unknowns" usually just becomes too hard.

Centers of Excellence

The most capable model is a center of excellence. It blends the best of a community of practice with a competency center. It centralizes resources into a shared services model while also taking responsibility for improving the broader organization's knowledge and capabilities in their targeted domain.

However, it also goes beyond this by adding:

- An explicit focus on (and a resource structure to support) communication and evangelization
- Ownership over defining a common value measurement framework
- Responsibility for actively finding opportunities to apply business analytics across the enterprise

At first glance they often look similar to competency centers. Both centralize skills and both support cross-functional business units within the organization. There is a difference, though. Where competency centers are usually fairly reactive, centers of excellence are highly proactive. Where competency centers are content to respond to business requirements, centers of excellence will actively find and deliver incremental value across the business. They provide support. However, they see their primary role as being an agent of change.

A second major difference is that they tend to have a broader focus than most competency centers. This is by no means guaranteed; some maintain a very narrow focus. When tasked correctly, though, there's a key driver that discourages too much specialization—a focus on value creation rather than centralizing skills.

Competency centers are traditionally defined functionally. They draw similar skills together to capitalize on economies of scale. By contrast, centers of excellence are focused on value creation and return on investment. They drive both economies of scale *and* scope. Because of this, they tend to require access to more skills than an equivalent competency center.

They normally maintain the full set of competencies needed in business analytics. They'll maintain people knowledgeable about data management, data science, value measurement visualization, and even how to embed analytics into operational processes. And, these all build on top of specialist skills such as risk management, predictive modeling, or other domains. In contrast, a competency center will often specialize in only a small subset of those competencies, dictated largely by those most required by their targeted focus. When correctly designed, centers of excellence represent extremely skilled, powerful, and valuable groups.[1]

The biggest disadvantage of centers of excellence is that they require a certain degree of scale to be successful. As will be covered in Chapter 7, it's almost impossible to find one person with all the skills needed to be successful in business analytics. Teams are the norm, and these teams need to have a certain degree of coverage across core roles and responsibilities if they're to be successful. This coverage requires investment, and most organizations need to have achieved a certain level of comfort before they're willing to take the plunge.

WHAT SERVICES CAN IT OFFER?

Having focus gives a group purpose. What it doesn't do is explain to the rest of the organization how to get engaged. To take advantage of a capability, people need to know what it is, how to use it, and how to get involved.

One approach is to simply throw a bunch of smart people together and hope for the best. While this works surprisingly well in smaller organizations, it rarely scales. The better approach is to make engagement easy through well-defined services.

Services are simply defined combinations of people, processes, and technology offered to customers with known outcomes. To create value, they support some form of business process. By reducing it to an offer with a clear value proposition, the group makes it easy to explain *why* and *how* other groups can take advantage of their capabilities.

Good support services cover the full gamut of platform support right through to identifying and delivering initiatives. Some are concerned with setting direction. Others are more focused on "keeping the engine running." Still others are focused on making existing things better. Operational excellence in business analytics brings all of these together in a way that drives a culture of continuous improvement and quality.

In defining these services, it's useful to consider the service design model described in Figure 5.2.

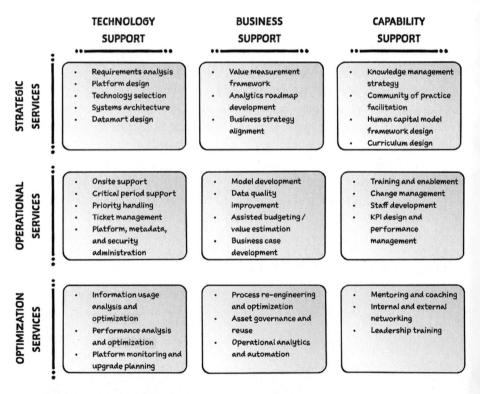

Figure 5.2 Service Design

Every business analytics service does one of three things. It helps set direction, helps deliver, or helps identify opportunities for improvement. These "activity" services provide support across the major aspects of the business—strategic planning, operational execution, and continuous optimization.

Every one of these services is focused on one of three things: technology, the business, or developing capability. The intersection of each of these helps define specific support services that help create internal or external value.

Not every organization has complete coverage across all of these areas. And, not all of these need to be offered by the same group. For example, technology support services are often managed by IT. Capability support may be managed by human resources (HR). Business support may be managed by a center of excellence. What's important is identifying gaps and closing them.

Strategic Services

Strategic support services help organizations define their direction and establish an execution plan. They help by providing the organization with the skills and support to create a roadmap, develop new capabilities, and provide governance or funding models.

Broadly, they focus on:

- Defining direction and funding execution
- Encouraging a consistent approach
- Developing skills and knowledge

At the strategic level, technology support services focus on developing a technology and data roadmap that map against current and future organizational requirements. Through understanding the organization's strategic direction, they aim to align and fund the organization's technology and data architecture. In addition to defining technology and data roadmaps, they also often provide a clear governance framework through which ongoing upgrades and feature requests can be captured, prioritized, and funded (often through a formal steering committee or the like).

Business support services aim to establish consistency in approach across initiatives. Through defining and encouraging adherence to common processes, they aim to make execution more efficient, consistent, transparent, and effective. Typical focus areas include defining and establishing a common value and effort measurement framework and helping to define the high-level milestones that every business analytics activity will follow. They're often focused on helping the business to develop an analytics roadmap that links tactical value into strategic differentiation.

Finally, capability support services revolve around fostering skills and cross-pollinating knowledge. Through establishing the right cultures and processes, they aim to shift skills from individuals to the organization, creating a self-sustaining culture that values business analytics. Common focus areas include establishing and running communities of practice, helping to define skills development roadmaps, developing knowledge management strategies, and developing curriculums that blend technical and domain training.

Operational Services

Operational support services help organizations deliver value and meet business outcomes. Rather than defining the "to-be" state and facilitating the change needed to get there, they focus on supporting current activities and ensure the business can do its day-to-day business effectively. They help by providing the business with the support it needs to do a variety of administrative and operational activities.

Broadly, they focus on:

- Monitoring existing activities
- Supporting operational execution
- Delivering operational outcomes

In this category, technology support services focus on ensuring the organization's technologies and data repositories perform against expectations and requirements. Through monitoring and resolving technology and data-related issues and requests as they're made, they aim to ensure high availability and prevent platform-related delays. Common services include onsite support, maintaining software currency and managing platform upgrades, priority and trouble ticket handling, metadata and security administration, and critical period support.

Business support services aim to clarify and assist with navigating and executing operationally related business analytics processes. Through providing specialist skills, they aim to help the organization move through each of the major phases associated with creating value from business analytics.* Common examples include helping to develop business cases, implementing value measurement and performance management frameworks, and defining change management and communication plans.

These also extend to data science. Through providing resources with specific competencies, they provide "overflow" support to overcome resource-related bottlenecks. Common services include providing data quality, model development, and analytical data management skills. The group might, for example, create a "model factory" to streamline and simplify the creation of predictive models.

Finally, capability support services help develop human capital and knowledge. They focus on training and enablement, support change management and cultural development, and link performance management to outcomes rather than activities.

Optimization Services

Optimization support services close the loop by helping to drive continuous improvement. They focus on identifying potential improvement opportunities and helping to maximize leverage of existing resources and/or assets.

Broadly, they focus on:

- Profiling existing approaches
- Identifying opportunities for improvement
- Assisting with process and asset reengineering

Technology support services in this context focus on profiling and improving the use of technology and data-related assets. Through profiling current usage patterns and identifying bottlenecks and inefficiencies,

---

*Defining the value, communicating the value, delivering the value, and measuring the value.

they aim to help the organization uncover common usage patterns across individuals and groups and facilitate improvements. Common services include helping to rationalize and streamline data management activities, benchmarking platform performance to identify and resolve bottlenecks, and identifying inappropriate or inefficient uses of technology.

Business support services aim to rationalize and streamline business analytics processes. Through mapping and analyzing existing processes across multiple business units, they aim to uncover best practices and replicate them across the organization. Common services include optimizing analytical processes (including information management, model development, and model deployment) and driving best practices in asset management.

Finally, capability support services assist by helping an organization to mature its abilities and become more proficient in business analytics. Through profiling current competencies across the organization and linking these to an agreed strategic plan, they aim to help the organization define specific actions to increase sophistication and experience in business analytics. Common services include facilitating mentoring plans and facilitating internal and external networking to promote cross-pollination of new ideas.

WHAT DATA DOES IT NEED?

Every organization needs to capture and manage the data that it creates. Regardless of whether it's a small business, a multinational enterprise, or a government agency, they all create and leverage data as part of their day-to-day operations. Bills need to be paid, customers need to be billed, resources need to be managed, services and/or products need to be delivered, and outcomes need to be tracked.

These largely transactional activities help the business operate. They also contribute to big data. There's value in the data, but thinking strategically requires the ability to step back from this transactional point of view and take a more holistic view at how the business operates. Rather than looking at whether an individual order has been fulfilled, decision makers might be interested in reviewing whether the average time needed to fulfil an order is competitive.

Taking this more strategic perspective requires the organization to view its data differently. This often involves consolidating information from multiple operational systems and transforming it such that the data is centered around the item of interest. For example, the organization might be interested in understanding overall customer experience and satisfaction levels. To determine this, they would normally be interested in how each customer interacted with the organization, how effective that interaction was, and how frequently the customer chose to interact in a particular way.

At the lowest level, this information is captured in systems that manage transactional interactions. To build this understanding, analysts might need to pull together data from its contact center, its online platform, as well as its order management system. These systems revolve around the transactions they manage. Respectively, they are concerned with issue tracking, content delivery, and order tracking. While each would capture information about the customer to different degrees, the comprehensiveness of this information will vary substantially. Getting to a strategic point of view involves drawing out the information of interest across the organization as a whole (the customer, in this case) and placing it front and center.

Conceptually, this may seem simple. What usually makes this process a bit complicated is that each of these systems usually has its own way of tracking interactions. For architectural and technical reasons, customer identification numbers may not match between systems. At a very simplistic level, one system may use the customer's full name and address as an identification, one may use the customer's identification number, and one may use the customer's online login details. Consolidating this information into a single view requires mapping tables that link this information together.

The rationale behind an enterprise data warehouse is usually that this information needs to be stored somewhere. Operational systems are normally designed to support a specific function rather than offer architectural flexibility, making them a poor landing point for the consolidated and aggregated data. Additionally, creating and storing these linkages requires processing power, capacity that existing operational systems may not have available. Rather than try to force an existing system to fit, most organizations choose to design a system that's fit for the purpose. And so, they establish a warehouse and start merging all the organization's information into a single environment.

This is a nontrivial task and takes years. And, that's assuming it ever really ends. Most organizations constantly generate new data as fast as their ability to capture information increases. Where they may start simply tracking which pages were viewed on their website, they may eventually get to a point where they track the mouse movements made by every customer across each page. With the amount of effort and expense organizations invest in creating this single, high-quality source of information, it's unsurprising that they try to encourage and sometimes force business analytics teams to use the warehouse and avoid interacting with the upstream source systems.

Unfortunately, this isn't always possible. Enterprise warehouses inevitably make a great starting point (and sometimes, if rarely, an ending point), but there are many situations where they simply do not contain the information the team needs to drive quality outcomes. In these situations, the team needs to source their own information and create their own information stores that go outside of the organization's agreed enterprise warehouse data model. Needless to say, this creates a great deal of tension—to the architectural team, it appears that the analytics team is duplicating large amounts of data. Even worse, data and systems architects often heavily underscope the amount of storage space needed by the business analytics team.

Understanding why this is the case involves understanding the limitations of a traditional warehouse when viewed through a business analytics lens. A team is only as good as the data it can source. And, analytical data often differs from typical warehouse data in four ways:

1. Granularity
2. Temporality
3. Comprehensiveness
4. Statistical completeness

Granularity

Advanced forms of business analytics require granular information, often to the degree of the original transactional measures. When this isn't available, many techniques become impossible.

Warehouses are expensive. They require high-performance technologies and large amounts of time to set them up and make them effective. This performance comes at a cost—highly available and redundant storage doesn't come cheap. Because of this, the designers need to compromise. The fastest (and most logical) way to reduce costs is to design the warehouse based on common requirements rather than comprehensiveness. It would be great to capture *all* of the organization's data in one location. However, most people just need a subset of the data that's theoretically available. A common starting point is simply moving from a product-centric point of view to a customer-centric point of view through creating a single view of customer.

To contain development, maintenance, and storage costs, the design team will limit source data capture to only what's necessary to achieve the required aggregations. They will then discard that same source data once they've met their requirements. This approach works well for relatively unsophisticated applications of business analytics such as reporting and dashboarding.

Unfortunately, it fails to work for more advanced forms of business analytics like predictive modeling and optimization. These rely on the use of statistics to identify patterns within large amounts of data and identify defining characteristics and relationships between elements. Usually due to cost constraints, this information is rarely kept in the warehouse. Capturing and retaining it can make a massive difference in the costs borne by the business.

An average-sized telecommunications company, for example, can generate a few terabytes of person-to-person transactional call information every month. All the majority of the organization usually needs, however, are some simpler measures such as the total number of calls each customer made over the last billing period. While the source data may be on the order of terabytes, the final derived information for all customers could be as small as hundreds of megabytes. Given the cost of highly performing and redundant storage, this represents a major cost difference. Because of this, the warehouse rarely contains the granular transactional information the business analytics team needs. The trick to ensuring *granular* analytical data is to make sure the original transactional data is available in some form if and when it's needed.

Temporality

One of the most powerful aspects of business analytics lies in its ability to identify dynamic characteristics rather than just static measures. Models can link behavioral and environmental changes to desired or unwanted outcomes and by doing so give the organization the ability to predict these outcomes ahead of time. Doing this requires having a record of information over time, and when this isn't available, understanding dynamic relationships becomes impossible.

The high cost of enterprise storage leads many architects and designers to try to contain costs in other ways. Another thing organizations often exclude is transactional history. Most business applications need either only current information or highly summarized year-on-year comparisons. While what happened four years ago may be of importance from an accounting perspective, it's rarely important in an operational context.

Excluding this historical data from the warehouse makes a great deal of sense given this intended use. If an organization holds a year's worth of information in the warehouse at the most granular level, holding five years' worth of information would require five times the storage. In assessing the cost and benefits of doing so, most designers conclude that retaining *all* data simply doesn't make financial sense.

Unfortunately, this information is tremendously valuable when it comes to more sophisticated applications of business analytics. Statistical modeling relies on identifying patterns through repetition. It's a simplistic example, but it's impossible to uncover a trend with two data points. Logically, at least three data points are needed to identify whether factors such as seasonality play a role in driving outcomes, and ideally more.*

Most warehouses are designed without these applications in mind and therefore lack sufficient history to enable more sophisticated forms of business analytics. Those that do have sufficient history usually lack granularity. The data usually still exists in source and financial systems; it's simply a case where the team is forced to go elsewhere for the information they need. The trick to ensuring *temporal* analytical data is to start collecting it early; once it's gone, it's gone.

---

*And, it must be said that three data points will create an extremely poor level of confidence!

Comprehensiveness

Another major advantage of advanced forms of analytics lies in its ability to incorporate vastly more information that we can mentally process. Models that include thousands of predictors are not unheard of. The best models leverage a wide variety of predictors to help link vastly different behavioral characteristics to target outcomes. Unfortunately, this breadth is rarely fully represented in the warehouse, largely due to the cost it would imply. When this information isn't available, the organization limits its ability to discover and exploit these relationships.

Humans are complex creatures—our behaviors surface in a variety of ways. If we're unhappy with our telephone provider, we may start testing other services such as online voice-over-IP offerings. Our phone usage might gradually decline over time as we favor videoconferencing services where possible. We may call their contact center to complain about our service, find out whether there are other services that might be a better fit, or enquire about our contractual commitments. And, as our contract comes up for renewal, we might start browsing through plans on the company's website, benchmarking plans against competitors.

Each of these actions is a leading indicator of churn—taken as a whole, they flag a customer at high risk of cancellation. Often, this panoramic data can be the difference between knowing what's going to happen and just making a guess. Statistical modeling would help the company not only quantify the degree to which each of these actions increases the odds of cancellation but also create a probability of cancellation for every single customer. Doing so, however, requires having the right data in the first place.

This true comprehensiveness is rarely available in the warehouse. Projects need constraints if they're to be delivered and warehouses are no exception. Trying to boil the ocean and include *all* the organization's data in the warehouse is usually uneconomical. To accommodate for this, the architectural team scopes their warehouse on current business requirements. Unfortunately, analytics is usually a voyage of discovery—it's hard to know what will be useful until one tests one's models with actual data. Inevitably, this means that there will be data of potential value to the analytics team that isn't included in the warehouse.

To be effective, the team needs to extract data from source systems, transform and cleanse it, and store it somewhere. This increases storage requirements and, if the reasons behind this are misunderstood, often creates a great deal of concern among the warehousing team. After all, the warehouse is usually meant to be the single source of truth. The trick to ensuring *comprehensive* analytical data is to give data scientists an area where they can incorporate the data they *need* rather than just the data that's *available*.

Completeness

Mathematical modeling can be a complex field. Many approaches are constrained by a variety of data requirements—some algorithms only work for binary (yes/no) outcomes and some need specific input data characteristics to work. When data isn't formatted or stored correctly in the warehouse, analysts may need to duplicate much of this data simply to enable them to do their jobs.

Having a single source of quality data is fundamental to running a business; it's impossible to make good decisions on bad data. Organizations often talk about this in terms of having accurate, complete, consistent, timely, and auditable data. This, however, creates subtle complexities. A great example is in tracking whether or not customers have opted in for email. Logically, one would think that there are only two possible answers: *yes* or *no*. In practice, there's a third option—they may not have answered the question yet. Representing this in data can become a rather complex question. On one hand, should "yes" and "no" be represented as text or as a number (1 and 0 respectively)? On the other, should a nonresponse be 0 or null (the absence of data)? Each of these is an accurate and complete representation of the data; it's simply a case of changing the storage mechanism. Despite being seemingly trivial, these decisions can have massive impacts on how easily teams can apply sophisticated forms of analytics.

Statistical modeling requires having numerical measures. If the fields are stored as free-text ("yes" and "no"), they need to be converted into a numerical representation before they can fed into a model. Usually, the field needs to be converted into a binary (1/0) representation where the 1s represent the occurrence of an event (having opted in, in this case). This involves extra effort and a complete replication of the field, necessitating more storage. This becomes even worse when the field in question has many levels (options). A retailer that classifies sales by sub-category may have hundreds of discrete values within this field, including "Female fashion—Skirts," "Furniture—Bedroom," and so on. To allow modeling, each of these is usually converted into its own binary field, exploding what was one field into hundreds.

Making things even more complicated is that some algorithms carry various data restrictions. A regression, for example, requires every field input into the model to be populated with a value of some form. Any records that are missing a value in any field are excluded. This creates a significant dilemma—in many situations, incomplete data is the norm. Some records will be missing because incorrect information was entered or because it simply wasn't captured at all. Having accurate data requires the organization to maintain these missing values—having a null field under "opted into email" may still be seen as being accurate and complete even if the field isn't populated. Unfortunately, this prevents all those fields from being used within regression and logistic regression models. To apply a broad set of algorithms, the analytics team need to repopulate these fields with "best-guess" values that are representative of the rest of the data while (hopefully) still preserving auditability by tracking which fields were original and which fields were statistically populated. This process is called *imputation*, and there are a variety of techniques that minimize the amount of statistical bias introduced by the replacement values.

Applying them usually involves duplicating even more fields; it's rare that the warehousing team will allow the analytics team to do wholesale field replacements in the single record of truth. This usually creates tension and substantially increases the amount of storage needed by the analytics team. Not doing so, however, substantially limits the ability of the team to generate accurate predictions when using relatively sophisticated techniques. The trick to ensuring *complete* analytical data is to educate and ensure that the organization's IT support group understands the difference *as well as* the reasons duplication is sometimes necessary.

NOTE

1. For a good overview on designing centers of excellence and how this links to organizational performance, see Aiman Zeid, *Business Transformation: A Roadmap for Maximizing Organizational Insight* (Hoboken, NJ: John Wiley & Sons, 2014).

CHAPTER **6**

Operating Models

nsight is easy; execution is hard. When it comes to big data and analytics, confusing the two is probably the single biggest reason organizations fail to see the returns they expect. At first, it seems counterintuitive. After all, the point of analyzing information *is* insight, isn't it?

The problem with insight is that in isolation, it's worthless. It's what you do with it that matters, not whether you have it. Markets are hard and, to coin a phrase, never bring a knife to a gunfight.

Everyone has *that* friend, the one who has an answer to everything, the serial entrepreneur, the one who would be rich if only someone would bankroll his great ideas. We love being around these people, but late in the night, after more than a few drinks, they're usually a bit of a bore. It's not that they're wrong; they're just missing the point.

Ideas are cheap. It's doing something with them that's the hard part. Given enough information, there's no end of interesting ideas a reasonably motivated person can come up with—ideas that, if fostered for long enough, sometimes germinate into potential innovations. Insight is the road that never ends; if you're not careful, the journey sometimes becomes more important than the destination.

There's always one more fact to find, one more way of slicing the data, one more information source, one more report, one more mashup. It's addictive. Discovery can be a dangerous siren; more than one explorer has become wrecked upon her shores.

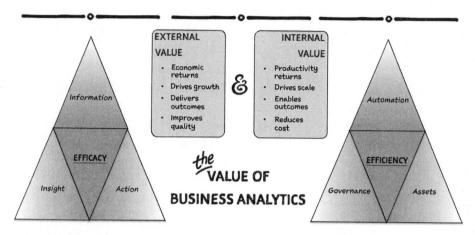

Figure 6.1   The Value of Business Analytics

The smartest group in the world is just another cost if they don't add value. And, while insight or efficiency is still a form of value, it's not the best type of value. The best teams excel in producing both internal *and* external value, as shown in Figure 6.1.

The true goal is *external value*. These are the outcomes that everyone *outside* the analytics group is happy to recognize. Usually tangible, they're normally closely linked to growth, improvement, or efficacy in some form. Common measures include revenue, profitability, or cost reductions. They're normally created through using analytics or big data to identify and deliver quality improvements in some form. It's created through sourcing information, generating insight, and acting on that insight to realize value.

On the way, those same teams need to create *internal value*. These are outcomes that people *inside* the analytics group see as valuable. Importantly, not everyone outside the group will always recognize these outcomes as being important. Sometimes intangible, they're normally closely linked to new capabilities, productivity, or efficiency. It's created through improving automation, managing intellectual property as assets, and ensuring governance processes are aligned against requirements.

While internal value *does* normally reduce structural cost in some form, the linkage between the outcome and the cost reduction is often unclear. For example, the use of prebuilt modeling processes might help teams do more work. Unfortunately, while productivity might help the organization avoid hiring people at some indeterminate point in the future, it's often hard to translate the opportunity cost savings into something an accountant will recognize. It's not impossible, but when it does happen it becomes external value.

The real value of business analytics comes through balancing these two forms of value. External value provides the return from big data. However, it's impossible without creating internal value on the way.[1] Doing this is impossible without having an operating model that aligns investment to outcomes, balances risk against reward, and gives each activity a "home."

This chapter tends toward the technical; it's intended for people who want to have a framework to map responsibilities between different groups in an organization. It covers three things:

1. What's the goal?
2. What's the enabler?
3. How does it create value?

The rest of this chapter will answer these questions and lay the foundation for effective delivery.

Readers interested in "getting to the meat" and reviewing the operating model are free to skip ahead to the section titled, "What Does It Look Like?"

WHAT'S THE GOAL?

Business analytics teams exist to create value. Like the alchemists of old, they are the modern-day magicians that are tasked with transforming data into value. Unlike the alchemists, though, their task is doable. Rather than transmuting lead into gold, it simply requires the ability to uncover advantageous patterns and act on them.

This is the core of *external value*. To create it, the team needs to get the right information, generate the right insights, and help the organization act on that insight to drive tangible returns.

Practical examples include:

- Using changes in calling patterns to identify people at risk of canceling their telephone services

- Mapping social-relationship information to identify and quarantine people at risk from known pedophiles

- Analyzing retail purchasing information to identify products that tend to sell well together and by doing so, change stocking patterns to maximize cross-selling products

- Modeling price sensitivity patterns to identify the ideal price to offer every customer to maximize margin while maintaining sales conversion rates

Despite how obvious this may be, surprisingly few organizations are any good at using big data to create external value. Rather than cultivating a forest, they focus on the trees and believe (falsely) that the forest is a natural outcome. Instead, to stretch the analogy, they usually end up with a series of disconnected hedges.

At a minimum, external value involves three activities:

1. Ensuring quality information

2. Generating knowledge through insight

3. Realizing value through action

Quality Information

Managing analytical information is mainly concerned with transforming source data into forms that are fit for other uses. There are four major activities that occur in this space. Of these, most organizations are only good at one. Developing an understanding of the other three activities is a key step in driving true economies of scale.

These four activities are:

1. Operational data preparation and delivery

2. Operational data quality

3. Analytical data preparation and delivery

4. Analytical data quality

The operational side of information management is usually well understood. Running a business requires many systems. Some provide transactional support—common examples include order management, case management, or customer relationship management. They provide the operational support that an organization needs to run its day-to-day operations. There are also normally a variety of systems that facilitate functional, business, and organizational planning.

While these use the information contained in the transactional systems, they require the information to be aggregated and transformed; knowing that a small can of beans was sold last Tuesday at 2:15 P.M. in store 31 is less useful in planning than knowing that over the last three months, total sales of beans in a particular geography has been increasing by 2 percent compound. Getting from one view to the other involves having a warehouse designer aggregate transactional sales by category, geography, and time period.

Sitting between all these systems is usually a warehouse that attempts to centralize all the organization's information in one location. Operational data preparation and delivery involves pulling all this information together and delivering it in the right form to the right system in the right order to make sure everything gets what it needs at the right time. This can be surprisingly complex, especially when one considers that different systems update at different times and, if the updates are not cascaded through the right systems in the right order, data can quickly get out of date.

Data modelers do this using a variety of extract, transform, and load (ETL) or extract, load, and transform (ELT) jobs, so named because they describe the major activities that need to occur. These are usually strongly governed and relatively inflexible—once defined, they will usually remain as-is until their source or destination data structures change. Every change carries cost; in practice, this happens as infrequently as possible.

Even unsophisticated organizations are usually still competent at operational data preparation and delivery, largely by necessity. Without the ability to manage data, it is usually extremely hard for decision makers to get any visibility over how the business is performing. There is an important caveat that goes along with this, however: simply getting the data into the right form has little relationship to whether the data is trustworthy or accurate. Over time, the organization starts to realize that despite having lots of data, most of it is relatively untrustworthy. This may be because of duplicate customer records (often because people use different addresses or change names) or it might be because front-of-house staff take shortcuts when entering information to speed up order processing (using all zeros is a common way of avoiding entering codes).

As organizations mature, they increasingly understand the importance of operational data quality and have usually established parallel processes to ensure the information used by the organization is correct. Common focus areas include data profiling and data cleansing. Again, these activities are ideally transformed into a variety of assets that have the potential to be deployed operationally.

This is a critical part of ensuring continuous data quality—when cleansing is treated as a one-off activity, information quality resumes its gradual decay over time once cleansing is finished. By operationally deploying these assets into ETL or ELT jobs, organizations can ensure that information is always correct and cleansed before it hits the warehouse or other destination systems. Organizations that forget this critical step and assume that cleansing is a one-off activity usually find that their information sources regress back to their original state.

At this point, organizations have a good grasp on operational data management as well as a set of high-quality and trustworthy information. However, there are still two other activities that, while similar, require a slightly different approach. Analytical data preparation and delivery shares many core requirements with its operational counterpart but extends these to include the need for a variety of statistical and temporal transformations.

A common example is the creation of "RFM" data that, for each customer, describes their most *recent* transactions (on a rolling basis), the *frequency* with which they transact over a certain time period, and a variety of measures describing their *monetary* spend (including their mean expenditure, maximum expenditure, and so on). This represents a fairly simple example—because the resulting tables are designed to be fed into a variety of models for training or scoring purposes, these additional fields can end up being highly complex mathematical derivations.

Analytical data quality is similar in the sense that it represents a superset of the requirements behind operational data quality. In addition to the need for profiling, cleansing, and matching, analytical data quality is also concerned with statistical characteristics such as completeness and importance. Because missing values can severely restrict one's choice of algorithms, increasing the "completeness" of data (even when it doesn't exist) is a major driver behind analytical data quality. Imputation is focused on generating replacement values without statistically biasing the original dataset or losing the importance of clearly distinguishing between "real" data and imputed data. Not all data is necessarily important or relevant when it comes to developing models. Identifying outliers and isolating the truly "important" information is another major source of analytical data quality.

Much like analytical data preparation and delivery, analytical data quality is often treated as a separate activity to operational data quality. While it may leverage a common technology platform, analytical data quality typically requires a higher level of statistical and mathematical knowledge in comparison to operational data quality.

The Knowledge of Insight

Given a rich source of data, generating insight is where most organizations start. Unfortunately, it's also where they tend to finish. This activity is focused on finding answers to questions or generally looking for interesting insights. Experience plays a massive role in this; knowing what to look for or how to apply the right techniques is critical. Because of this, it's usually highly iterative and weakly defined.

Generating insight from big data requires four activities: exploratory analysis, exploratory data preparation, insight generation, and asset development.

Exploratory analysis usually starts without a defined endpoint in mind—the main objective is discovery. It can range from being as simple as browsing through data to get a feel for it, to using cross-tables and correlation plots to look for interesting relationships. Usually, the analysts doing the exploration have little idea what they're looking for upfront. All they have is some data, a lot of curiosity, and possibly some hypotheses. Unsurprisingly, this is an area where data scientists add tremendous value.

Exploratory data preparation usually involves extracting and structuring data to support model development or report creation when the used cases are ill-defined or unknown. It is a highly iterative process that is repeated until the end-state can be defined. A good example involves trying to find the right data structures to help a particular business unit make better decisions. They might not know what they need. However, they'll almost always know it when they see it.

A common pattern might involve extracting a set of data, deriving a series of measures such as the average sales over a particular time period, and then socializing the results with them and recutting the data as necessary. Another common example involves developing the input tables needed to develop a model. While the analyst may have some assumptions or beliefs as to what behavioral characteristics drive particular outcomes, it's not until they can test those assumptions with a statistical model that they can validate or disprove them. And so, they will repeatedly create and test these tables with new derived fields until they finalize their model.

On finding what they're looking for, analysts will move on to developing models or reports. The tables created during exploratory data preparation are used as inputs to generate insights and answer questions. The major difference between this and exploratory data analysis is that during this activity, the analysts have a defined objective. They may be trying to identify the major reasons behind customer churn or they may be trying to identify the levers that have the greatest impact on getting someone back to work after a major occupational injury.

Finally, these insights are ideally transformed into assets in their own right. Unsophisticated organizations miss this step entirely. Instead, the analysts give these insights to decision makers as indirect sources of information. Rather than build a recommendations process that tracks action, they'll just pick up the phone and give the answer or send through a spreadsheet. This creates two problems.

First, while the team can ensure that the information is delivered to the right decision makers, they have no way of ensuring that the information was actually used. With no tracking mechanism in place, they've no way of knowing the value of the information.

Second, the team is limited by their ability to manually communicate their findings. Every time they generate new insights, they need to spend more time making sure the right people get the right information. This heavily limits their ability to capitalize on economies of scale and reduces business analytics into an interesting, if somewhat erratic source of minor value for the organization.

Transforming insights into assets involves taking insights and turning them into objects that can be accessed by other people or systems. Most people are familiar with the idea of automated reporting. However, fewer people are aware that more advanced forms of analytics such as predictive modeling or optimization can use the same approach.

In this situation, the models themselves can be turned into a series of formulas that the organization can deploy into operational processes. However, doing so requires analysts to convert their personal skills into automated processes, often facilitated by purpose-built software. Getting to this point requires both automation and supporting systems that allow the use of analytics within operational processes.

The Need for Action

Realizing any real value requires one more step: taking action on insight to drive a specific outcome. There are two major activities that go along with this: presentation and decisioning. Presentation is primarily concerned with getting relevant and concise information in front of decision makers while decisioning is primarily focused on automating operational and microdecisions across the enterprise.

Most organizations are fairly mature when it comes to establishing and managing structured presentation (or business intelligence) technologies. However, it's also true that many organizations could benefit from better visualization practices—creating a report and creating an *effective, relevant,* and *concise* report are not necessarily the same thing. Regardless, presentation on its own has one fundamental flaw—it is impossible to directly link the insight to the outcome. The information contained within the report or dashboard may well have influenced the behaviors of the decision maker, leading to a better outcome. Or, it may not have—it's possible that on that particular occasion, they decided to follow the advice of their hairdresser!

While it's not always the case, presentation systems usually rely on the assumption that it's up to the decision maker to synthesize all the information made available to them and from that, make an independent decision. This decision happens independently of the presentation system, breaking the link between insight and outcome and making it extremely hard, if not impossible, to quantify the value of business analytics in a true accounting sense. Instead, the organization needs to quantify value by making broad assumptions about how information is used.

This dilemma also highlights one of the reasons why it is often so hard to objectively quantify the value of business intelligence. Few will disagree that having immediate access to better information drives better decision making. However, it's also true that most struggle to explain how much decisions have improved once the organization has access to better information.

Decisioning systems strengthen the link between insight and outcome by moving away from insight and toward recommendation. They blend a variety of rules and models to either provide specific recommendations to decision makers or automatically make decisions on behalf of the organization. These decisions drive specific outcomes such as flagging potentially fraudulent transaction, identifying whom to contact to drive down churn, or recommending the most appropriate program to an individual in need of social services. If these decisions are acted on, the organization can quantitatively determine the value of the action. If they are ignored or overridden, the organization can track the value creation or destruction of the alternative decision. By doing so, the organization directly links insight to outcomes and gains the ability to quantify the value of business analytics.

It's important to note that closing the value chain does not necessarily require measuring outcomes in a comprehensive way—it simply requires actioning insight. This seems like a small distinction, but it's an important one. Many organizations successfully operationalize their insights and drive real value without operationalizing the corresponding value measurement processes. Instead, they manually determine the benefits they've derived as a one-off activity. Establishing a comprehensive and automated value measurement framework is one of the factors that distinguish organizations at level two from those at level three of the cultural imperative.

WHAT'S THE ENABLER?

Big data gives organizations countless opportunities to create value. Unfortunately, there's only so many hours in a day. Without becoming more efficient, there's just not enough time to solve every problem and realize every opportunity.

Productivity enables external value. Unfortunately, productivity alone does little to the bottom line unless the organization uses that efficiency to reduce structural cost through downsizing or otherwise reducing operating costs. It does, however, enable organizations to do more with less. This is the main benefit of internal value; it's the organization's ability to scale through being efficient and responsive.

Internal value comes from:

- Improving the efficiency through automation
- Reusing analytical assets
- Understanding the need for governance

The Efficiency of Automation

Automation is possibly the single biggest enabler for productivity. This happens in two ways:

1. Automating information management assets
2. Automating analytical assets

The cornerstone to this approach is moving away from manual activities. Copying and pasting data within Excel is a common example of a manual activity. Every time new data arrives, the analyst needs to spend time massaging the data into the right shape. It can't be automated, it's highly inefficient, and it carries extremely high support costs.

By comparison, code-based approaches (such as using SQL) create an asset, albeit one that still carries a fairly high support cost. This asset can be embedded in other systems and executed without any manual interaction. They do allow automation. However, their efficiency depends on the skills of the person who created them.

Purpose-built tools take this to another level. They usually offer the best solution, albeit at the highest entry cost. They're often built to expressly facilitate automation. They are tailor-built with efficiency in mind and usually reduce support costs by providing prebuilt migration and asset management functions.

Analytical assets are no different. Exploratory data analysis tools can also usually be used to build models. These models are accurate but need to be used interactively. Some tools offer some degree of scripting or coding. These help transform the model into an asset, but they also increase support costs and, unless skills are common in the organization, link the asset to the person who created them. They're also not always compatible with existing IT assets, forcing redesign work.

More sophisticated organizations create dedicated operational analytics and decision orchestration platforms. These carry the highest upfront costs but also reduce support costs, increase efficiency, and enable systems-level integration and automation.[2]

Most organizations are well aware of the benefits of automation. Common examples include operational data management, reporting, and sometimes operational data quality. Warehousing and business intelligence are mature disciplines. Because of this, the benefits of automating data management and reporting processes are well understood.

Unfortunately, the same can't be said for many of the assets that link into decisioning systems. Efficiency comes from establishing the frameworks, processes, and architectures to support automated scoring and decisioning. In practice, this may take the form of the following:

- Scheduled scoring processes that automatically take recent behavioral information and generate customer-level probabilities that indicate propensity to churn.

- Automatically monitoring transactions in real time to identify potentially fraudulent activity based on a series of rules and propensities and, if flagged, automatically actioning the transaction with the fraud team and putting a hold on the credit card.

- On becoming an outpatient after an emergency ward presentation, dynamically assessing medical history and prescribed medications to identify whether entry to a consultative care program would reduce the odds of a future representation at the emergency ward and, if so, assigning a case worker and scheduling the first visit.

In each of these cases, a variety of analytical assets are deployed operationally to automatically make business decisions based on the most recent known and predicted behaviors. This approach not only links insight to outcomes but also drives significant economies of scale. Rather than investigating accounts based on a random sample, the organization can assess every single transaction individually.

Arguably more than anything else, it's automation that transforms business analytics from something that augments existing processes into an enabler for competitive differentiator in its own right. Without it, scale is impossible.

Reusing Assets

Once these assets have been created, they need to be managed. This usually happens in two ways:

1. Managing information assets
2. Managing analytical assets

It's important to remember that this activity spans the full breadth of analytical assets produced by the organization. Common examples include reports, models, information management processes, datamarts, and all their associated documentation. While there is no reason that these couldn't (or shouldn't) be combined into one asset repository, current skills, practices, and technologies tend to make this harder than it needs to be.

Efficiency comes from:

- Tracking these assets in a centralized, metadata-driven system
- Understanding how well they're performing
- Understanding how much value they're creating
- Understanding how frequently they're used
- Managing them through their full lifecycle

Creating any type of asset takes time and effort. It incurs real costs. Building a house involves a wide variety of specialist skills, including builders, electricians, and plumbers. It also requires significant capital investment for bricks, electrical equipment, and concrete. On top of that, it takes time.

Information assets are no different. They require specialist warehousing, modeling, and business skills. They require capital investment for the right information management, model development, and decisioning tools. And, they also take time to develop, time that carries an opportunity cost.

Similar to how we monitor and manage our return-generating real-world assets, we also need to monitor and manage our information assets. Real-world assets depreciate. Once built, the house inevitably suffers normal wear-and-tear that eventually requires maintenance costs. Some of the structural characteristics may not be appropriate for changing environmental conditions. A clay bed may contract during a period of dry weather, putting cracks into the walls and requiring a minor rebuild. Keeping on top of these and ensuring the asset is performing well is an obvious good practice.

In an ideal world, information assets carry none of this depreciation. As long as things remain constant, the asset will continue to perform exactly as designed. We don't, however, live in an ideal world. Customers change over time, rendering the assumptions that underpin the asset inaccurate. Business models change, rendering the rules that drive decisions irrelevant. And, people sometimes deliberately change their behaviors to avoid detection. For example, criminals change their patterns as soon as they know what intelligence agencies are looking for. Staying on top of this asset depreciation is a key component of achieving best practices in asset management.

While automation is a key part of being able to monitor assets efficiently, it's more than that. Efficiency and productivity comes from *not* reviewing assets. When the measures are set up correctly, the organization need look only at assets that are underperforming or underused. By grounding the philosophy in value rather than effort, the organization can reduce maintenance costs and increase time available for better value-creating activities.

The Need for Governance

Coordinating all the groups involved in business analytics can be extremely challenging. The greater the overhead needed to coordinate activities, the harder it is for organizations to leverage business analytics as a real competitive rather than just a useful source of insight.

Productivity and efficiency comes from:

- Defining an engagement model that identifies the handover points between individuals
- Establishing standardized development and deployment processes

Getting this right helps drive process efficiencies, ensure quality control, and simplify the application of competencies across new problems. It also ensures that governance is tailored appropriately. Too much, and innovation suffers; too little, and operational risks increase.

It's a key part of an effective operating model. The major focus in this area is on managing workflow and facilitating collaboration and, just like integration and asset management, this occurs at two levels:

1. Coordinating the development of analytical assets
2. Coordinating the deployment of analytical assets

As with asset management, there is no reason why both of these activities can't take advantage of a common technology platform and management approach. It's important to remember, however, that while the vast majority of their requirements overlap, the level of emphasis placed on specific requirements varies between the two.

Achieving best practice within this process requires at a minimum:

- Establishing a clear operating model that outlines roles, responsibilities, and handover points
- Documenting and following standardized processes
- Having well-defined points of ownership with the power to make decisions
- Ensuring a high degree of quality through explicit quality control activities

Unclear processes almost always create highly variable outcomes and process inefficiencies. It's hard for an organization to drive continuous improvement when everyone follows a different process. Some people will naturally do things more efficiently than others. Unfortunately, when everyone does things differently, it's almost impossible to replicate those efficiencies. Having standard processes not only increases agility through making sure everyone has clarity on how to execute but also ensures that everyone benefits when team members find new efficiencies.

This does not necessarily mean that activities need to be defined to the lowest level of detail possible—a certain degree of pragmatism and realism needs to be applied when working out an appropriate level of granularity. It's also true that too much rigidity stifles innovation; when people aren't given the freedom to experiment, improvements tend to be the first thing that suffers.

Underpinning these processes are roles and responsibilities. To be effective, everyone must be crystal clear on what they are responsible for delivering as well as when they need to get involved. This helps provide certainty as well as reduce transaction costs. By linking roles to activities, the workflow system itself can automatically notify stakeholders when their interaction is required. If a champion model has been submitted by an analyst, the next logical step would be for the information management team to deploy that model into production and validate the predictions against the original model. Ideally, the system itself handles all the necessary notifications based on a combination of asset registration or workflow and process management.

Finally, effective governance requires a high degree of quality control. When it comes to dealing with operational systems, repeatability and transparency are critical. Every process must be exhaustively tested prior to moving it into production lest it fail and cost the organization real money. Minimizing risk involves ensuring that standard tests are applied, making sure that appropriate signoffs are followed, and ensuring that outputs and predictions are the same in production as in development. While the checks will vary between information assets and analytical assets, the need for a high degree of quality control is a constant.

HOW DOES IT CREATE VALUE?

The fastest way to discourage innovation is to make it hard. Everyone has a day job; if you're trying to get people to go above and beyond the call of duty, you need to make it easy. As covered in the last two sections, there are many moving parts in creating value. And, each of these parts involves multiple parties. Because of this, simply setting up a group isn't enough; it needs to be accessible, responsive, and valuable. If it isn't, it'll fail.

The best answer is one that blends flexibility with rigor, aligned against an operating model that gradually transitions from exploration into execution. Rather than building the approach around the funding model, the funding model should be dictated by the operating model.

The Wheel of Value

In moving from insight to execution to improvement, every organization needs to follow the *wheel of value* and go through six key stages, as shown in Figure 6.2.

Value only ever comes from the ability to execute. In cases where this involves coordinating multiple parties, this is only possible when

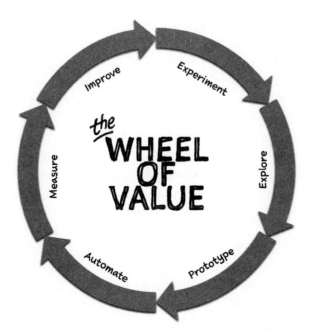

Figure 6.2 The Wheel of Value

there's a clear operating model. A well-defined operating model ensures that:

- Processes are aligned to support agility through prototyping, with "process hardening" happening only once solutions have been validated.

- Insight is acted on, thereby allowing the potential for better outcomes and impact.

- Measurement supports self-awareness, improving focus in the right areas and allowing for pragmatic effort and investment prioritization.

- Institutionalized learning processes enable and support growth and continuous improvement.

One of the biggest advantages of big data lies in its ability to expose "unknown unknowns." By mashing up novel combinations of information, data scientists can discover insights that the organization may have never even considered. Experimentation usually takes place in the absence of a defined business problem.

Once a business problem has been defined, the organization moves on to exploration. The business faces a challenge that requires some form of analysis. Again, this is deeply within the realm of the data scientists. Through blending qualitative and quantitative evidence, they seek to validate or disprove some hypothesis. It might be as simple as testing whether some customers prefer email over phone contact. It might be as complex as identifying the root cause for revenue leakage within a highly complex supply chain and manufacturing process.

This, along with experimentation, is the core of analytics as most think of it; it's complex, it's scientific, and it's usually highly numerical. It's also highly uncertain; data scientists rarely know the answer before they start. At best, they'll have the experience to know what will likely get them to the right answer. In practice though, it's usually a voyage of discovery, one where novel insights frequently abound.

Because of this, it's characterized by weakly defined processes. Success usually comes down to the creativity and capability of the individual. While some control measures can and should be put in place, at best they're usually guidelines and milestones. While everyone should still be working from common technologies and data sources, there's still a strong need for flexibility. The fastest way to inhibit outcomes in this stage is to mandate heavyweight and standardized processes. Kill creativity and you kill the Golden Goose.

Eventually, this creative process generates an answer. It may not always be the answer people were expecting, but it's an answer, nonetheless. What might have started out as a fraud investigation might eventually turn out to be a sales opportunity. Knowing the answer is half the battle; to make the answer worth something, it needs to be acted on. The best approach to doing so is to integrate the analytics into operational processes.

For example, unhappy customers rarely enjoy being sold to. By incorporating customer sentiment into the recommendations it makes, the organization can better decide whether to focus on sales or service by customer. Rather than sell to an unhappy customer, it might be better to tell them ways that they can better use their existing services. And, rather than tell happy customers about the benefits of the services they've subscribed to, it might be better to take the opportunity to offer other services that they'll be even happier with.

This represents a change in delivery. Insights usually come from a creative process, one involving weakly defined processes. To automate these processes, they need to be strongly defined. Without a series of steps that involve clearly defined inputs and outputs, it's impossible to turn these manual processes into automated processes.

Unfortunately, the people with the skills to create these insights are often not the people who are best placed to create these automated processes. This doesn't represent a lack of vision of understanding; it's simply the reality of an increasingly fragmented skills base created through hyper-specialization. Building the skills required by a high-performing data scientist can take a decade or more. Building the skills required by a high-performing enterprise architect can equally take a decade or more. Rather than setting the unrealistic goal of hiring someone with perfect skills, it's usually easier to split functions between prototyping and automation, thereby increasing the size of the available labor pool.

Prototyping involves building an asset that is characterized by:

- *Algorithms and logic* rather than guidelines and weakly defined processes
- A high degree of *encapsulation*, in that the asset is portable and can be handed to other people or systems for controlled use without breaking functionality or outputs
- A high degree of *abstraction*, in that the asset takes a known and finite set of inputs and delivers a known and finite set of outputs without the user needing to understand the internal complexities of the asset

Exploration and prototyping require agility and flexibility. They're focused primarily on user acceptance. Requirements are rarely known up front and delivering to business requirements is a highly iterative process. Because of this, while these prototypes reflect an accurate representation of the logic needed to deliver the outcome, they are rarely:

- Scalable
- Robust
- Ready to be integrated with operational systems

Automating these assets typically involves going through strongly defined development, test, and production processes that progressively:

- Optimize their underlying logic to achieve higher levels of performance
- Validate their results against expected results
- Integrate their logic into operational systems while ensuring business continuity and overall systems stability

Once automated, these assets provide regular recommendations to management, operations, and front-line staff through expected delivery channels. Automation is frequently the domain of IT and tends to focus more on unit and integration testing. The goal at this point is not to create something new. It's to take what's already been created and make it bulletproof.

Closing the loop involves ensuring that the impact of these recommendations is understood and that actions (or inactions) are adjusted to support continuous improvement. This involves ensuring that activities are measured and evaluated and, based on results, adjusted to support continuous improvement. These carry through the final stages: measurement and improvement. All parties have a role to play in these stages, focusing on their personal areas of expertise.

By mapping roles, responsibilities, and funding models to the six stages of the "wheel of value," organizations make it clear how insights will eventually move into production. They make it easy for other business units to get engaged. And, they provide clarity on where the handover points exist and what's expected at each point. A major point of competitive differentiation comes from reducing the time it takes to move through this entire cycle. The faster the wheel, the greater an organization's ability to out-think, out-act, and out-learn its competitors.

When this operating model is broken, the business inevitably experiences four pains. First, insight without action destroys value. Having too much insight without the ability to act on it creates confusion and introduces delays through "analysis paralysis." Typically, it eventually leads to organizations rejecting the use of their information assets. When it becomes too hard to leverage quantitative insight in any meaningful way, people will revert to gut-feel and subjective opinions.

Second, action without insight is guesswork. Insight can stem from qualitative or quantitative sources and can be intuitively or analytically based. Critically though, actions that are not based on clear linkage to supporting evidence are no better than guesswork and, more often than not, lead to suboptimal outcomes.

Third, outcomes without measurement prevent improvement. When the effectiveness of actions in driving outcomes or impact is not measured, organizations have no way of knowing what is or is not working. This actively inhibits improvement.

Finally, measurement without learning creates stagnation. Measures are worthless unless they are actively used to drive better behaviors. It may be that particular services are known to have minimal impact on getting long-term beneficiaries off the welfare system. This knowledge does little unless it is put into practice and operational staff are discouraged from offering those services.

Ensuring Sustainability

To be sustainable, every group needs to cover its costs. Unfortunately, this sometimes acts as a major barrier to the organization getting engaged. It'd be nice to offer services for free. Unfortunately, everything costs money and data scientists aren't cheap. Changes to operational systems or data warehouses are even more prohibitive. It's not unheard of for a single data feed to cost over a million dollars in internal resourcing costs.

Every group is established as either a cost center or a profit center. Cost centers are covered through a defined budget with no expectations that they'll cover their costs. As a shared service center, they support the business and are very easy to engage with. They also struggle to justify ongoing investment; to an accountant, they're still a cost. Profit centers need to be self-sustaining. Through negotiation, transfer prices, or direct cost recovery, they need to be able to demonstrate their contribution to the organization's bottom line. While they're often proactive, every integration they have with another unit "costs" money. As such, while they rarely struggle to get investment as long as they can demonstrate financial performance, their constant focus on cost recovery can act as a disincentive for other groups.

This seems to force an impossible choice. If the group tries to recover its costs from the start, it'll compound cultural resistance with financial resistance. No one likes being asked to pay for something upfront where the value is not necessarily known yet. Unfortunately, analytics is mainly about dealing with uncertainty. However, never recovering *anything* greatly limits what the team can achieve. Making changes to operational systems costs real money and without this funding, it's impossible to embed analytics in operational processes.

Clearly, neither model is more effective than the other; each offers different advantages and disadvantages. The mistake most organizations make is to assume that it needs to be one or the other. By starting with the funding model rather than the desired outcomes, they make it that much harder to succeed.

The best solution is to align the funding approach against each activity's objectives. Early on, the net should be cast as wide as possible. While the expected value from any given project is usually quite low, some will offer significant value. These need to be identified and validated if a case is to be made for change. Once validated, the

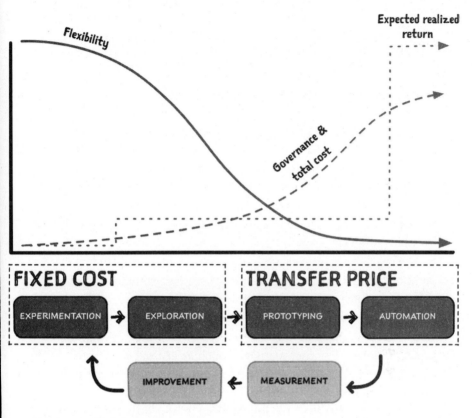

Figure 6.3 The Return Cycle

expected return should be significant enough to justify the investment that will be needed to change operational processes.

Following the trajectory of expected value creates the process described in Figure 6.3.

During early stages, the main objective is simply to determine whether a solution exists and, if so, whether it's feasible to develop. Rather than create barriers to adoption or innovation at this point, it's better to make it as easy as possible to engage with the group. By treating the people who support exploration as a cost center, other groups are free to engage without having to allocate budget or otherwise reprioritize their activities. Flexibility is key during this stage and as such, simply defining the engagement approach is usually enough. Activity and focus are best managed by prioritization, often supported through an oversight executive committee comprised of key senior stakeholders from the group's customers.

If there's merit in investigating whether it's worth converting the results of exploration into an operational process, that same group can assist with feasibility and prototyping. Agility and relevancy are key during this stage and, as such, methodologies such as Agile are well suited. Even better, the target result of this process should be a clear understanding of what the value of the change would be to the business. This helps build the business case and justify more direct and significant funding. Activity and focus are again best managed through prioritization, again through the oversight management committee.

Converting the prototype into a robust operational process is where the real costs start to mount. It's also where the real value of business analytics starts to emerge. Because of this, it also makes sense to treat the group responsible for automation as a profit center with their time accounted for either through cost recovery or direct recognition via a true or shadow profit-and-loss statement. Efficiency and repeatability are key during this stage and because of this, service design approaches such as the IT Infrastructure Library (ITIL), software development methodologies such as the waterfall method, and project management methodologies such as PRINCE2 are well suited. Activity and focus is managed through direct investment and program of work management.

There's good reason to separate exploration from execution. By having an investment model designed to both encourage use *as well as* support return, business analytics becomes self-funding without unintentionally establishing barriers to adoption. The goal is to make it self-sufficient and profitable, not just a cost center with no clear direction.

NOTES

1. For a far more comprehensive review and explanation of these concepts along with how to quantify them, see Chapters 4 and 6 of Evan Stubbs, *Delivering Business Analytics: Practical Guidelines for Best Practice* (Hoboken, NJ: John Wiley & Sons, 2013) and Evan Stubbs, *The Value of Business Analytics: Identifying the Path to Profitability* (Hoboken, NJ: John Wiley & Sons, 2011).

2. For more detail on the use of operational analytics and decision orchestration, see Chapters 6 and 9 of Evan Stubbs, *Delivering Business Analytics: Practical Guidelines for Best Practice* (Hoboken, NJ: John Wiley & Sons, 2013).

CHAPTER 7

Human Capital

C hange is inevitable and business analytics is a profession of change. The domain has and will continue to change—as our data grows exponentially, the real game is moving away from sheer brainpower to being able to harness and reduce complexity. Having the right answer is only the first step. Without the right supporting systems to act on that answer, it's all wasted effort.

That doesn't necessarily preclude sophistication or highly advanced analytics. What it does instead is encourage focus on developing the right competencies, tasking people with the right objectives, and structuring the organization in a way that allows it to foster, retain, and develop talent. By focusing in the right areas, the leadership team can hire the right people, establish the right incentives, drive efficiencies, and nurture the right behaviors.

One of the reasons it's so hard to find the right people is because of the breadth of the field. Business analytics is a spectrum that ranges from relatively simple information management to highly specialized fields such as operations research or machine learning. Assuming people with different skills are substitutable just because they work in "analytics" is a recipe for disaster. Much like building a house requires more than just a carpenter, most of these skills are not interchangeable.

That in itself is a challenge—without the right domain knowledge, hiring someone with highly specialized experience can be a shot in the dark. Complicating things further is that while analytics tends to focus on hard skills, business analytics requires both hard *and* soft skills. As a profession, business analytics is primarily about blending change management skills with technical domain knowledge. To help with building human capital, the rest of this chapter focuses on three things:

1. What capabilities do I need?
2. How do I get the right people?
3. How do I keep them?

Reducing uncertainty during the hiring process is difficult. Luckily, though, there are a few things to be aware of that can help improve the odds of getting the right person. Getting off on the right foot starts with knowing what you're looking for. The rest of this chapter will answer these questions and lay the foundation for skills acquisition and development.

WHAT CAPABILITIES DO I NEED?

Data scientists have been getting a lot of interest. There are many reasons for this, not the least of which is the amount of chatter about big data. However, it's more than just a title. There's a very real need to describe in a concise way the difference between a statistician or analyst and someone who practices business analytics. In markets characterized by imperfect information, buyers and sellers often develop signals that help communicate relevant information in a concise (and often difficult to replicate) way. Being aware of this and taking advantage of it can make the difference between hiring the right or wrong person for the job.

Numerical analysts have been described by a variety of titles. Depending on the context, industry, and organization, they've been called applied statisticians, data miners, predictive modelers, risk analysts, or just simply quantitative analysts. The field is broad, but these roles consistently exhibited some common patterns:

- A focus on numerical analysis in some form
- Specialized in technical skills
- Strong background and focus on theoretical knowledge
- Ability to generate and communicate insight

These are critical in generating insight. Business analytics, however, goes beyond this—it also requires the ability to:

- Emphasize recommendations over insight and outcomes over analysis.
- Define processes based on an organization's ability to execute, not on what's possible.
- Create repeatable processes rather than doing independent, discrete, and one-off activities.
- Understand and apply organizational psychology and influence.

For an organization hiring someone to drive business analytics, these differences can make or break a project. To see why, consider Figure 7.1.

As covered in the previous chapter, value comes from using information to generate insight and take action. This value needs to be aligned against strategic priorities and the organization's unique business model. However, action is impossible without change. And, change requires a reason to act. The value needs to be understood *and* communicated. And once delivered, the only way to fuel more change

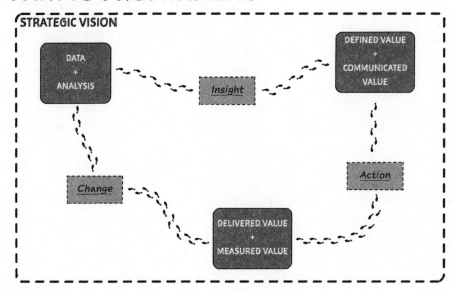

Figure 7.1 The Path to Profitability

is to build trust through measuring that value and demonstrating that everything promised was delivered.

These are very different skills. Getting insight out of big data is impossible without access to high-powered analytical capabilities. However, getting an organization to change is impossible without the ability to communicate, sell, and build trust. This, at its most basic, is the difference between a *data scientist* and a *value architect*. And, organizations interested in maximizing their return from big data need *both*.

For those hiring, advertising a role for a "data scientist" rather than an "applied statistician" can help communicate the different focus and intent. However, if they're unaware of the importance of change in the overall process, they can quickly find that what they got wasn't what they were looking for. These differences also need to cascade down to the job description and be made obvious—while it won't stop the wrong people from applying, it will help improve the odds of getting the right person.

Data Science

Generating insights from data isn't a new profession. Historically called *quants*, *statisticians*, *analysts*, or even the now-quaint term *computers*, organizations have been using data-crunchers to create competitive advantage for centuries. In fact, it sometimes comes as a surprise how *long* the profession has been around. It's arguable that Bletchley Park managed to shorten World War II by years through their cryptographic analysis.[1] Even Guinness, the well-known brewer, was using analytics at the turn of the twentieth century to create competitive advantage.[2]

Still, there are some differences. First, data science is more than just analytics; it blends communication skills with information management and experimental testing knowledge. While the difference may seem small, a key part is the scientific mindset data scientists bring. They emphasize testing and validating a hypothesis using big data rather than simple exploration or statistical reporting. Good data scientists excel in simplifying the complex, always striving to get to the core of the problem.

While they demonstrate an academic or scientific mindset, their goal is to solve the problem, not necessarily expand the boundaries of knowledge. In that sense, their focus is very much applied rather than theoretical. Characterized by curiosity, they get excitement out of answering the *why* and working out the *how*. Faced with impossible challenges, they'll look for a way to overcome them rather than accept them.

Second, they have the ability to work with big data. At a minimum, they're completely at home with "large data." More typically, they're comfortable with big data in its purest sense. Unstructured, high-velocity sensor data presents an exciting challenge to them. For experienced data scientists, experience working with petabytes of data simply justifies membership to the club, not recognition.

Finally, they are highly multifunctional. They draw their knowledge and experience from multiple disciplines and often, multiple domains. Many have experience in domains as diverse as linguistics, graph theory, and unsupervised machine learning. Programming is a given, as is knowledge of statistical methods. This forms the heart of one of their greatest strengths—their ability to draw from multiple schools of thought. They have an almost-supernatural ability to see the patterns among industries, cross-referencing and using their experience to solve diverse problems using common skills.

Competent data scientists are hard to find. As in every growth industry, many claim the titles that seem to carry the greatest remuneration. Unfortunately, just because someone has the title Data Scientist on his resume doesn't necessarily mean he is one.

Value Architecture

Data scientists are a key part of the picture. However, they're not the answer on their own. Insight without the ability to get the organization to act on it is wasted potential. The biggest mistake organizations often make is to assume that their data scientist can do *everything*. In some rare cases, she can. Usually though, getting value out of big data and business also requires someone to focus on selling the value of change.

Like the opposing forces of *yin* and *yang*, data scientists need their counterpart if they're to create value. Too much insight can be detrimental; faced with a data deluge, the worst thing one can do is to use that data to generate even more data! Left alone, many data scientists will fly beyond their organization's ability to comprehend the value of what they're doing.

The answer isn't to stop them from being smart or innovative. Instead, it's to make sure that they're complemented by someone focused on helping the organization transition and change. This is a different skill set, one characterized by *value architects*. These *theotors*, literally the "gods of twist," are experts in change. Almost *actipreneurs*, they are experts in making sure insights are acted on to drive real benefits.

Unlike data scientists, they care a bit less about the insight. Instead, they care about the organization's ability to realize *value* from that insight. They're often more passionate about innovation and getting the business to change for the better than they are about the specifics of the "how."[3]

Communication is obviously a key part of this. However, their skills go beyond those of a data scientist. Their role is that of a true change agent, one who understands how to define, persuade, and drive organizational transformation. While they may not have the analytical capability to mirror the best data scientists, they're unparalleled in getting the organization to change the way it operates.

Change starts with a sense of urgency. Value architects help the organization understand what the change is worth. They help the organization navigate the path to get there. Finally, they use those successes to fuel the next round of change. Value architects are the link that enables the organization to get value out of the analytical capabilities. While some data scientists are *also* value architects, most aren't. The goal of a value architect is to move the insight through to action and, eventually, change. They're also the key to unlocking longer-term differentiation. They ensure a focus on linking tactical gains into strategic benefits.

The Power of Both

Left alone, few analytics teams are good at change management. That's not a criticism—if their primary objective is to generate insight, there's little need for skills that don't support that goal. Business analytics, however, is about driving change. And so, part of establishing an effective business analytics team involves augmenting the analytics team with business analytics skills.

Given most data scientists are focused on data, detail, and mathematical creativity, it's rare to find one person who has all the right skills. Unfortunately, without someone to evangelize and drive real change, the investment most organizations make in data scientists goes to waste. Establishing a strong capability means having a plan to acquire *both* types of skills, not one or the other.

Good value architects are an even-rarer breed than data scientists. They draw heavily from knowledge of operational analytics, change management, and strategic planning. As Figure 7.2 shows, they complement the skills of the data scientists and together, they are the lynchpin to unlocking value and enabling innovation from big data.

The most effective business analytics teams structure themselves to support two somewhat different objectives. On one hand, they provide enough role coverage to span the entire analytical lifecycle from information management to operationalization and value measurement. On the other, they also understand that delivery, while essential, is only part of the picture. Delivery also requires a defined opportunity, broad stakeholder support, and the right frameworks in place to ensure every initiative represents a connected steppingstone to true competitive differentiation.

In many ways, these represent two sides of the same coin: one is focused on value creation while the other is focused on value identification. These are tightly interdependent—without its counterpart,

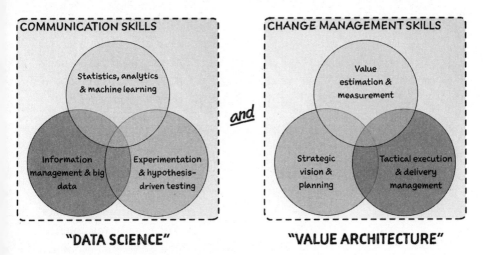

Figure 7.2 Data Science vs. Value Architecture

each is largely ineffective. Delivery without an opportunity usually regresses to exploration and research. An opportunity without the capability to deliver is simply a good idea. The best teams have a blend of resources and responsibilities that support both.[4]

Rather than simply accepting the team's environment as a given, the most effective teams play an active role in transforming the organization, focusing on:

- Proactively identifying opportunities to drive value through business analytics
- Driving and managing change
- Ensuring consistency in execution and measurement across the organization

This reflects a very real move toward playing a proactive role in driving transformation. Instead of being fearful of change, the team embraces it and, by developing skills in change management, helps the organization move toward best practice. They each focus on different things, as shown in Figure 7.3. The heart of business analytics is change. This requires both an answer as well as a reason to change.

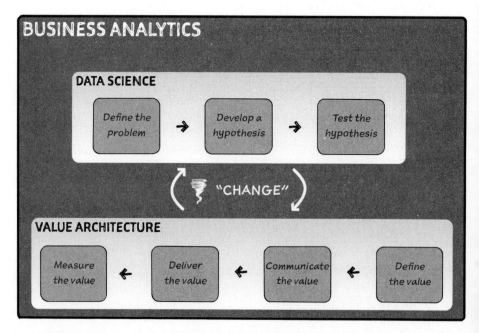

Figure 7.3 Data Science Combined with Value Architecture

Data scientists concern themselves with the answer, value architects with the reason to change.

Together, they link insight to value. Often, they form a partnership to lead a broader team. These roles do not necessarily map one-to-one with individuals. People in smaller teams may play more than one role. Critically, though, an effective team has coverage across both these activities to some degree. When there's insufficient coverage, the odds of success drop substantially.

HOW DO I GET THE RIGHT PEOPLE?

It shouldn't be surprising that some teams are just better than others. While it's true that technology, data, and process can all influence success, it's also true that these pale in comparison to having the right people.

This isn't unique to business analytics; it's a well-documented phenomenon that shows up across every industry sector and discipline. Fred Brooks found that their most highly performing programmers were 10 times more productive compared to their average peers.[5] Robert Glass set this even higher, suggesting that the most productive programmers were *up to 28 times more productive* than their peers.[6]

Great results require great talent; Steve Jobs often spoke of his need to hire "A" performers.[7] This is equally true in business analytics. While performance obviously varies, the most capable firms are able to achieve a level of productivity (as measured by outputs or financial impact) often over an order-of-magnitude higher than the second. This is despite often having an order-of-magnitude fewer data scientists employed.

The SMART Model

There's clearly a difference. And, it's not surprising that given a choice, it everyone wants more of the first type of people and fewer of the second. The obvious question is, how do you identify them?

High-performing people display three different types of capability. At a minimum, they need to know how to do their job. Hard skills allow entry; applicants need to understand their tools, apply the scientific method to data analytics, and be competent in interpreting their results. Validating these skills is fairly straightforward; because they're

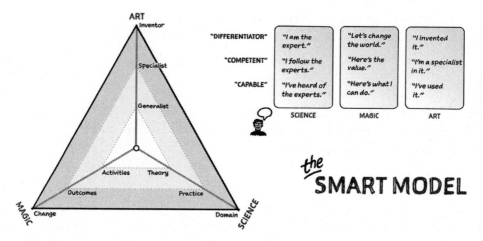

Figure 7.4 The SMART Model

precise, it's a case of testing knowledge. To this end, many interviews focus on case studies, artificial problems, or experiential validation. Unfortunately, it's here where most interviews stop. And, these skills are the *least* important when it comes to success.

The trick to developing an effective team is in recognizing that not everyone needs to be expert in everything. Some people will naturally develop into analytical experts. Some will become change agents. Others will become experts in driving business value. Having the right framework makes it easier to hire better people as well as develop internal talent. Luckily, there's a simple way of identifying the right people. Figure 7.4 shows a technique to ensure high-quality human capital.

Art

The ideal data scientist knows everything. She can make magic happen. And, she has that "art," the knowledge of how not just to do the job but to excel in it. We'd all love to hire that person. Realistically, though, finding the perfect person is impossible. Instead, it's easier to make sure that in aggregate, the team has access to all the capabilities it needs. While no one person might be perfect, the whole may yet be greater than the sum of its parts.

On the scale of effort, the *art* is the easiest to develop. It simply requires the right training and exposure combined with the right attitude. Gaps can be filled by on-the-job training, courses, or higher education.

The starting point is having access to generalist experience. While the person may have held many functional roles or responsibilities, at this level he has rarely encountered the same problem multiple times. Regardless of whether one is considering analytics, big data, or even managing innovation, challenges are solved from first principles and efficiency is relatively low. The bare minimum of competence is having the hard skills necessary to "do the job."

Given enough time, individuals face the same challenges repeatedly. Exposure causes their functional knowledge in specialist areas to increase, thereby increasing their efficiency through sheer experience. They understand best practice and hold to it.

A small set of people go beyond this. Drawing on their deep functional knowledge, they transition from being a specialist into an inventor. Rather than following best practice, they define it, often relying heavily on emerging technologies, knowledge, or networks. They ride on the crest of the wave, leading the industry as a whole.

Hiring an inventor is intuitively attractive. Unfortunately, in isolation these skills rarely correlate well with long-term success. Competency always has a role to play in the problems people can solve. However, just because someone *can* solve a problem with the skills he has does not necessarily mean that he *will* solve the problem.

This is often one of the reasons "B" performers end up hiring "C" resources. Without intuitively knowing how high performers are different from average performers, those doing the hiring need to rely on quantitative and objective methods to shortlist candidates. And, there's nothing more explicit than stating and evaluating technical and nontechnical requirements for a role. Knowing how to do the job plays an important role in eliminating bad candidates but it helps little in differentiating the good from the great.

Skills are important, but without the maturity and science to go along with them, they don't guarantee success.

Magic

If having the right degree and the right experience says little about a candidate's ability to succeed, what else is there to go on? Beyond being able to know how to do their job, high performers also demonstrate different behaviors. They approach their work from a perspective of "getting things done," and more often than not, understand the importance of quality. Their motivation is aligned with the organization's higher intent, their focus is on making a difference, and they deeply understand the organization's high- and low-culture characteristics.[8] This is the *magic* that turns someone from an expert into an enabler for change.

Needless to say, these skills are far harder to identify and evaluate without prolonged exposure. They're also the hardest to develop in a structured way. Unfortunately, they're also the most important factor in determining success. It's for good reason these are often referred to as "soft" skills. They come with *maturity*, something that's hard to train. To be effective, much of the effort focused on organizational change and human capital development *needs* to be focused on reinforcing and developing these skills. Coaching and mentoring are the main ways of developing these skills.

In practice, these differences span a broad spectrum of cognitive, behavioral, communication, and motivational factors. More than anything else, it's these characteristics that distinguish "A" performers from their counterparts. And, whether it be intuitive or deliberate, "A" performers often have an innate ability to identify people with similar behaviors. As managers or leaders, they either shape and enforce their culture around them or they leave; nothing frustrates a high performer more than being around incompetent or unmotivated people.

Getting people with the right soft skills is essential. Of course, the core challenge is that those same soft skills, by their very nature, are exceedingly hard to pin down. Consistently, though, high performers in business analytics tend to exhibit one or more of the following behaviors. They:

- Are effective and often passionate communicators and evangelists
- Have a deep and often diverse platform of hard skills to draw on
- Maintain a focus on value and outcomes rather than insight and answers
- Demonstrate a balance of creativity in problem solving with pragmatism in practicality of execution
- Understand the importance and role of culture and change management in driving outcomes

It's useful to view this *"behavioral" spectrum* across three levels, each of which builds on the previous. The starting point is understanding the importance of delivery. Without activity, nothing happens. The bare minimum of competence is ensuring that the job "gets done." Usually, they benchmark their professional success on whether they've met their performance metrics.

At some stage, most individuals start to question the impact their activities have on the broader business. When this happens, some make the intuitive leap to understanding the importance of outcomes rather than effort. Their attention often moves to demonstrating return, measuring outcomes, and building a culture focused on value creation. They benchmark their professional success on the value they have created.

Again, a small set of people go beyond this. Rather than being content with their organization as it is, they see the potential of what it could be. Their focus shifts toward change and evangelism and their effort moves toward organizational transformation. They benchmark their professional success on the degree to which they've changed the world around them.

Science

The need for experience and soft skills is not unique to business analytics. Whether they're employed in consumer goods, the public sector, or any other industry, high performers everywhere demonstrate these characteristics. Where business analytics differs from many other disciplines is the need for cross-functional knowledge. Without *science*, the best skills in the world are just theoretical.

Analytics is a technical discipline based on rich theory. However, it can't happen in a vacuum; to create value, it needs to be applied to a business problem. And, solving this problem most effectively requires domain knowledge. This spectrum of *science* is the final dimension that differentiates high performers from average performers.

At the lowest level is theory. This often spans a wide range of disciplines, including mathematics, computer science, machine learning, and the scientific method. The bare minimum of competence within this dimension is having a sufficiently deep prerequisite level of knowledge to start experimentation. While individuals may have solved problems in academic or theoretical contexts, they lack the "battle experience" of solving the same problems in environments clouded by politics, poor data, and constantly shifting organizational priorities.

Over time, this theory transitions into practice. They apply their skills to real-world problems and, by doing so, build an understanding of how abstract mathematical or computational processes can be applied to business problems. These individuals have the knowledge *and* ability to solve business problems using analytics.

Yet again, a small set of people go beyond this. Building on their raw analytical knowledge, they gain an understanding of their organization's business model. They make the leap from practice to domain expertise, bridging the gap between deduction and intuition. Rather than having generic analytics skills, they straddle the gap between mathematics and business, having the ability to play the role of both the analyst *as well as* the business representative. They understand the constraints the business is operating under, the outcomes it is trying to drive, and all of the low-level intricacies that might prevent it from realizing the opportunity.

HOW DO I KEEP THEM?

The difference between a team that retains its high performers and one that lets them churn is like night and day—there's nothing that undermines an organization's ability to capitalize on business analytics like losing the team.

There's good reason for this. As covered in Chapter 2, the labor market will continue to tighten. Still, it's important to remain pragmatic. The fact that skills are scarce shouldn't be a reason to live in fear. The mantra for the future is, achieving excellence requires *developing* excellence.

Retention is critical because it takes time to understand an organization's processes, information sources, and business models. On one hand, new starters face a variety of technical challenges. They need to understand what information is captured and available, how trustworthy that information is, as well as how best to take advantage of their technology landscape. However, this is only a small part of their overall learning curve. Because business analytics is fundamentally about driving change, they also need to understand the organization's political landscape, business model, and culture. This doesn't come easily—it takes time to absorb.

Because of this, employee turnover is the bane of every team. Losing the wrong people can set a team back by months. These pains are particularly acute in a business analytics team. It's not uncommon to see new hires be almost totally unproductive for anywhere up to a year while they come to terms with an organization's unique characteristics. An analyst is only as good as her ability to understand the data she is working with.

Given that a team should ideally be creating value in under a 12-month horizon, delays caused by employee turnover can totally undermine a team's success. Retention is always difficult. However, there are some useful guidelines to keep in mind. Effective leaders:

- Understand their team's worth
- Keep things interesting
- Develop first, and hire second

First, keep on top of what you're paying. Wage inflation is likely to continue over the next decade. However, the equally harsh truth is that not everyone is worth what the market is willing to pay for their skills. Shortages have a tendency to raise prices equally across the board, not just for those who deserve them.

On one hand, being price competitive is mandatory. On the other, so is balancing the opportunity cost of replacing existing skills with new. Long-term success requires developing a very real and frank understanding of how effective every resource is when benchmarked against market averages and paying rates to suit.

Second, match interests to activities. For some people, stability and repeatability is attractive. They value developing deep skills in a specific area. Others value innovation and breadth of experience. They value constantly facing new challenges and exploring the unknown. Retaining a good team often comes down to understanding what people enjoy and ensuring that the roadmap aligns with their interests.

This isn't to say that the tail should wag the dog. The roadmap should always be defined to drive value and competitive differentiation. However, the breadth of what's possible is enormous, and wherever it makes sense, this roadmap should capitalize on the team's interests.

Finally, don't assume that extending capabilities requires going external. Many believe that good analysts can't be trained; the subject matter is sufficiently complex that practitioners require higher education simply to create the right foundations. However, this misses a key difference between advanced analytics and business analytics. Within business analytics, it's possible to create significant value using anything from relatively simple techniques to the most sophisticated. This *can* be developed, especially through coaching or mentoring. Developing maturity is something that's best done under the guidance of a leader with vision and understanding.

Of course, there's always the attraction of bringing in "new blood." Sometimes, this is a good thing. However, because business analytics is so heavily aligned against an organization's business model, a cornerstone of this is a strong understanding of the business. Relying on employee turnover to build skills is limiting; the best teams fully understand their business. And, the best way to do this is to develop first and hire externally second. The obvious exception is when the team moves toward more and more sophisticated techniques. Often, these require heavily specialized experience that can only be found in the market. However, this should be the exception rather than the norm.

NOTES

1. T. M. A. Lomas and Computer Security Group, "The Influence of ULTRA in the Second World War" (interview by Harry Hinsley), Computer Laboratory, University of Cambridge, Nov. 26, 1996, www.cl.cam.ac.uk/research/security/Historical/hinsley.html (accessed Apr. 21, 2013).

2. Joan Fisher Box, "Guinness, Gosset, Fisher, and Small Samples," *Statistical Science* 2, no. 1 (1987): 45–52.

3. Evan Stubbs, *The Value of Business Analytics: Identifying the Path to Profitability* (Hoboken, NJ: John Wiley & Sons, 2011).

4. For a full list of the roles that normally fall within a business analytics team along with typical hiring patterns, see Chapter 3, Evan Stubbs, *The Value of Business Analytics*.

5. Frederick P. Brooks, *The Mythical Man-Month: Essays of Software Engineering* (Reading, MA: Addison-Wesley, 1975).

6. Robert L. Glass, *Facts and Fallacies of Software Engineering* (Boston, MA: Addison-Wesley, 2003).

7. Walter Isaacson, *Steve Jobs* (New York: Simon & Schuster, 2011).

8. For more detail on organizational culture and how it often affects value architects, see Chapter 5 in Evan Stubbs, *The Value of Business Analytics*.

FOUR

Making It Happen

I n Part One we looked externally, considering how our world is changing. In Part Two we looked internally, considering how we can change ourselves. In Part Three we looked around us, considering the ways we can make things better.

In this final part we look to the future. We complete the journey and bring it all together into a model that enables innovation.

8

Innovating with Dynamic Value

Success is impossible without knowing what it is you're trying to achieve. Ironically, one of the biggest challenges in getting value from big data is usually working out where to start. Given a smorgasbord, the worst thing to do is to try to eat everything at once.

As a rule, we're a species that enjoys self-improvement. Faced with a problem and motivation, most of us would rather solve it than live with it. We may not all have the ability to tear down a car for servicing, but given the right set of skills, the right opportunity, and the right motivation, anyone can innovate.

Consider James, our well-intentioned if slightly erratic innovator. In his journey to monetize his organization's data assets, he recognized fairly early that analysis alone wasn't enough. He sold his vision on the back of innovation and, one way or another, he had to deliver it. Unfortunately, he failed to understand what he meant by "innovation." Because of that, many of his successes in his first year were underappreciated or outright overlooked.

Innovation sounds sexy. It's also pretty amorphous; if it were easy, there probably wouldn't be so many books on the topic. The best starting point is to remember that there's a difference between *innovation* and *invention*. Invention is unique; it represents the original creation of something new. By contrast, not all innovations need be completely novel. In fact, the opposite is normally true—most innovations are simply improvements to existing knowledge, processes, or products.

Invention can only happen once for a given concept. Innovation based on that invention, however, can happen millions of times; innovators improve inventions and often re-purpose them. Dr. Martin Cooper may have been the father of the mobile telephone. However, it was HTCT, TMN, and Eircell (among others) that took that invention and changed the way payments were made to reinvent the composition of their industry through prepaid mobile plans. Great success comes from either; just because it's not groundbreaking doesn't mean it isn't innovative. The trick is in viewing innovation not as a one-off activity but as a repeatable process.

This chapter brings everything together. It links big data, analytics, and human capital into an *innovation engine*, one that creates *dynamic value*. It covers:

- The innovation cycle
- The innovation paradox
- The secret to success: dynamic value
- The innovation engine
- Reinventing the rōnin

THE INNOVATION CYCLE

Innovation, at least conceptually, is actually surprisingly straightforward. There needs to be a good idea. There needs to be a way of translating that idea into a solution to a specific problem. There needs to be a way of making that idea a reality. These are simple steps, but they're deceptively hard to do. Many ideas get lost because there isn't a clear channel to take advantage of them. The vast majority of innovations go nowhere—it's easier to think than it is to do.

This innovation cycle is shown in Figure 8.1. Big outcomes always start with ideation, the process of generating ideas. These ideas are then made real through invention or innovation, usually accompanied by a great deal of experimentation and effort. And finally, the successful prototypes are commercialized.

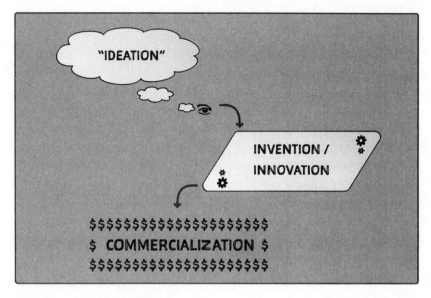

Figure 8.1 The Innovation Cycle

Business analytics isn't any different. Generating innovation from big data is straightforward, if not necessarily easy. It starts with an operating model that:

- Encourages and rewards a culture of creativity, curiosity, and ownership
- Translates the innovation cycle into a practical process
- Prioritizes effort and investment based on value creation, not activity

Get those right and while not guaranteed, innovation and invention at least becomes achievable.

As with many things, innovation is rooted in culture. Anyone can innovate as long as they're given the freedom, flexibility, and tools to do so. Big data represents a treasure-trove of fertile ground for potentially innovative novel data mashups, insights, and solutions. Unsolved problems often lead to invention. And, coming up with interesting ideas or problem definitions can often be as easy as encouraging cross-pollination of experience and knowledge through internal rotation or external networking. What's standard in one industry may be ground-breaking in another.

To come up with good ideas, people need to feel comfortable doing so. Ideation is impossible when people are punished for being creative and having curiosity. Equally, motivation is impossible without some degree of ownership and some form of reward, financial or otherwise. Organizations that refuse to acknowledge internal challenges are a classic example of this.

The manufacturer discussed in Chapter 3 refused to recognize that many of their core problems came not from external issues but from internal inefficiencies. A significant proportion of their business model revolved around importing foreign products and distributing them domestically. Unfortunately, their volumes were highly volatile; if they ordered a thousand of a particular item in any given month, in three months they might have received anywhere from five hundred to two thousand.

Among many other challenges, the organization had developed a self-reinforcing culture of accepting the status quo and discouraging curiosity. Every attempt by new hires to investigate and resolve the source of this uncertainty was discouraged in favor of the existing process. In most cases, these new hires eventually left for more supportive cultures, further reinforcing the dominant culture. The true irony is that that same organization not only had the data to solve their issues but was already using relevant simulation and forecasting techniques elsewhere in the business to solve the same problem in an unrelated area.

Eventually, this culture was a contributing factor to killing the organization. Constant profit erosion and customer dissatisfaction led to declining market share. After repeated cycles of downsizing and redundancies, they passed the point of no return.

THE INNOVATION PARADOX

Encouraging ideas represents the starting point. If relevant and feasible, some of these ideas may generate true invention. PageRank, an algorithm developed by Larry Page and Sergey Brin while at Stanford, used large amounts of data to rank information importance based on link popularity. That single invention ended up spawning one of the world's largest companies, Google. More importantly though, not every innovation is the same. The best way to improve the ratio of effort to success is to understand that for the vast majority of organizations, certain types of innovation are inherently incompatible.

Some of us are dreamers, entranced by the world that might be. Others of us are doers, interested in improving our existing world. Some straddle the two, equally at home in both worlds. We're inherently flexible; we adapt to our social structure, our surroundings, and even our desires.

Organizations don't work this way. People need to be aligned. There needs to be direction. They require structure to succeed; by definition, without structure there is no organization. There's simply a collection of individuals.

This structure carries significant advantages. It distributes authority and streamlines decision-making processes. It makes it easy to mobilize a large number of people around a common goal. And, when operating effectively, it offers efficiencies that would be otherwise impossible to achieve individually regardless of knowledge, skill, or experience.

Unfortunately, these advantages do not come free. Larger organizations face increased transaction costs; coordinating thousands of people is far harder than coordinating 50. Bureaucracy and diseconomies of scale have ground more than one organization to a halt. Equally, directed authority is a benefit *and* a curse. It helps drive efficiency and experience. Being able to focus in a specific area helps build capability. It also constrains focus to the scope of authority. In most situations, this unknowingly eliminates one of two types of innovation.

To understand how this works in practice, consider the different operating models of two groups in an organization. On one side is a team responsible for various business-as-usual activities, many of which could be improved in countless ways through reusing the organization's data and existing analytics capabilities. On the other is the executive team, driven by the shareholders to ensure growth and commercial success. Both are aligned around organizational success. The form that success takes, however, might be slightly different.

To the team, success might be defined by efficiency. Efficiency will improve profitability, thereby delivering shareholder value. One source of innovation in their mind might be the use of Six Sigma techniques or analytical process automation. To the executive team, however, success might be defined through reinvention. If their market is mature, opportunities for growth might be limited. Innovation in their mind might stem from leveraging existing data assets to move into new market segments, diversifying their business and opening new growth avenues.

Both are legitimately innovation, and both are valuable. There is a difference, though: one is *evolutionary* innovation and the other *revolutionary* innovation (or, in author Clayton M. Christensen's terminology, *sustaining* and *disruptive* innovation[1]). To the team, innovation might come from chasing continuous improvement. Toyota, through their application of *kaizen*, became tremendously successful taking this approach. Constant and continual improvement over a sustained enough period of time can create deep pricing and quality differentiation.

To the executive team however, innovation might come from doing things fundamentally differently. They might be more interested in questioning their existing business models and potentially actively disrupting their own markets. Reinvention is a powerful force and organizations like Apple are famous for actively cannibalizing their own markets before others can. This, too, can create deep differentiation, through developing inimitable goods, capabilities, or processes.[2]

Both are tremendously valuable. Critically though, it's almost impossible to charge any single person with doing both. Even though he may have the capability and interest in doing either, asking him to do both amounts to asking someone to both improve what he's doing as well as stop doing what he's doing. This forces cognitive dissonance, the outcome of which can only be either ignoring one approach or becoming paralyzed with indecision.

The business *requires* repeatability and efficiency. However, revolutionary innovation *requires* questioning the status quo and "breaking the rules." Even worse, the second is an active threat to the first. Large organizations are built to sustain and perpetuate their business models. Successful revolutionary innovations *force* change and disruption. Without forethought or a plan, being put in charge of "disruptive innovation" is often a poisonous pill. When left unmanaged, the conflict between evolution and revolution almost always ends with casualties; the organization fractures until the individuals charged with revolutionary innovation are driven from the company. All things being equal, in a battle between the two, business as usual *always* wins.

A prime example of this conflict involved a publisher facing market disruption. Like many traditional publishers, they were under threat from the twin forces of "free" content and the move to digital media. Their revenue model was heavily biased toward advertising—even though they operated on a paid subscription basis, the subscription fees they received barely covered the cost of paper and distribution. Once the fixed costs of journalists and plant were taken into account, their subscriptions alone would have left them bankrupt in mere months.

Their profitability depended on advertising. And, the rates they could charge from advertising were based on their subscriber numbers. In effect, they didn't sell content; they sold eyeballs. Their customers were not their readers; they were the companies interested in paying for advertising space. As business models go, theirs was a fairly standard one in the industry. It did, however, create an interesting dynamic when it came to inventory management.

For retailers, the ideal stock management model is to have no products left on shelves at the end of the replenishment period. They keep stock levels at a minimum, freeing up capital and improving liquidity. By shifting the focus of the business to replenishment rather than space management, they improve sales velocity and revenue generation.

For publishers, having no products left on the shelf at the end of the replenishment period is actually a significant problem. Because their revenues were directly tied to the number of people they could get their product in front of, having empty shelves meant that they might have been able to sell *more* product had they not had a stock-out. Given they were already carrying the significant fixed cost of a large distribution network with a daily replenishment schedule, the incremental cost of an additional newspaper was negligible compared to the advertising losses caused by a smaller readership.

Managing this need to maximize readers had created all sorts of complexity. In their need to drive continual efficiency and support innovation, their distribution teams had developed countless complex rules to take into account the difference between weekday and weekend editions, the effect of rain in different suburbs, and even the effect of different covers on purchasing rates.

The rules were astonishingly specific. For example, they'd found that covers with busty women tended to sell better in specific suburbs on specific days of the week unless it was during school holidays! To take advantage of these variations on sales volumes, they'd built a tremendously complex set of rules that would determine the correct number of papers for distribution to a specific news outlet the night before deliveries were to take place.

When I dealt with them, the business had fractured into two different sets of opinions. The bulk of the business believed in their current model. While it was becoming increasingly unmanageable, they believed that a more scalable technology platform designed for managing rules would help them extend their exception-based management approach down from a suburb level to a news-agent level.

There was also a small set of individuals who believed that they were going about this the wrong way. Rather than rely on what was an ever-growing team of distribution managers, they felt that they might be able to leverage their data assets to *automatically* generate accurate forecasts. They'd built prototypes that had shown that relatively unsophisticated stochastic forecasting and simulation methods could generate forecasts as accurate as their existing rule set. Importantly, though, those same forecasts had only required a team of five to develop and manage in comparison to the existing 80-strong distribution team.

Both groups were innovative. The distribution team were experts in evolutionary innovation from data analysis. The "new guard" were able to demonstrate the power of revolutionary innovation through automated analytics. Unfortunately, the organization ended up compromising on only evolutionary innovation. Because they couldn't manage the internal conflict between the two groups, their core business won the battle and they missed a spectacular opportunity.

THE SECRET TO SUCCESS: DYNAMIC VALUE

The trick to enabling innovation from big data is not to fight against these inherent conflicts but instead to embrace them. Authors Vijay Govindarajan and Chris Trimble talk of the "performance engine," the core of the business that seeks operational excellence and ongoing profitability.[3] This engine, while an excellent optimizer, is generally poor at revolutionary innovation. It's the reason that most organizations are actively allergic to things that challenge their existing business model. Anything that threatens the status quo triggers an immune response that rapidly acts against disruption. This isn't because people don't have the skill, the knowledge, or even the interest. It's because the organization's operating model emphasizes discipline and repeatability over disruption.

Big data is an enabler for both evolutionary *and* revolutionary innovation. To realize both, organizations need to establish separate teams with different operating models. Analytical capabilities must be embedded within business-as-usual operations. Without access to these skills, organizations miss opportunities to realize incremental improvements through business analytics. Visualization, exploration, and process modeling through techniques such as Six Sigma can help identify and deliver countless improvements.

To ensure long-term success, organizations also need to be willing to challenge and potentially reinvent their existing business models. Big data, when harnessed, can transform organizations. In some cases, this might involve expanding into parallel industries, such as in the case of retailers using their knowledge of customer purchasing patterns to expand into coalition loyalty programs or banking and financial services. In other cases, it might make entire areas of the business redundant due to analytical automation, such as in the case of the publisher discussed earlier.

The challenge, naturally, is to develop a holistic operating model that maintains a healthy dynamic tension between operational excellence in the context of organizational stability and disruptive innovation in the context of reinvention. This is easier than it would appear once the building blocks are understood. Overlaying these different types of innovation on the wheel of value gives the operating model and organization design shown in Figure 8.2.

Ideation is primarily a cultural challenge. People need to feel safe in sharing their ideas. The leadership team has a critical role in creating this culture, whether it's through reward structures, recognition, or even simply a "good ideas" register. Good ideas on their own are worth

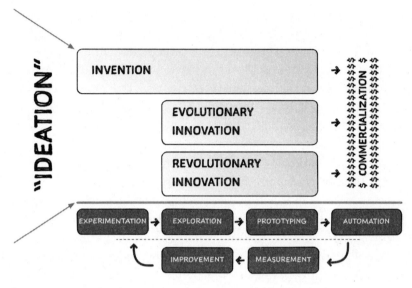

Figure 8.2 Dynamic Value

little, however; they need a home. Rather than try to task everyone with doing everything, it's better to charge different groups with different objectives.

Invention is often best left to dedicated research and development teams. There are good reasons for this. For example, invention usually has very different goals from the performance engine. Not all inventions will turn profitable. Instead, a common measure of success is the *volume* of novel and relevant outputs generated by the group. Because of this, putting too much emphasis on profitability through the pure research and development stage can act as an inhibitor for invention. The team becomes so focused on demonstrating return that creativity and ingenuity suffer.

Evolutionary innovation is often best left to the performance engine. Usually, they have direct responsibility for ongoing commercial success. They often measure success through very tangible financial measures such as profitability, cost, or revenue. And because of this, they understand their business better than anyone else in the organization. This places them in the best position to deliver continuous improvements. Not only do they usually have the best perspective on where the opportunities lie but they also have the best understanding of the real-world challenges that might prevent good ideas from being executed.

Finally, revolutionary innovation is often best left to a separate, dedicated team. Their names vary; often named SWAT or Tiger teams, their focus is on developing creative solutions to challenging problems. Usually multidisciplinary, they are granted significant freedom and encouraged to challenge and question assumptions. By nature, they are usually in direct conflict with the performance engine. Because of this, their sustainability is heavily dependent on the support they receive from their leadership team. They often also act as the bridge between the research and development team and the business as a whole, looking for opportunities to apply novel inventions in a commercial context.

Managing the dynamic tension between these groups is both the challenge and the solution. Tension lies at the heart of innovation. Too little and the organization becomes complacent and lazy, comfortable in the belief that it's doing the right thing. Every empire has eventually ended, from the Babylonians to the Romans to the British. Whether it's measured in months or years, complacency is inevitably the start of the end in a competitive market.

However, too much tension and the organization becomes paralyzed by political gridlock. Each of these groups usually offers a wildly different perspective on what's important to the business. And, each is usually right in their own way. Groupthink is a dangerous force and too much time spent in a self-reinforcing culture can lead to irrational or inefficient decision making.[4] In the worst cases, the chasm between these groups becomes so significant that it fractures the organization.

The trick to managing this tension is to create counterbalancing forces that sustain and temper. Creating tension is as easy as establishing different groups with directly conflicting objectives. While there should be no overlap in the *outcomes* owned by each group, there are significant benefits to having these outcomes being somewhat contradictory.

For example, every bank maintains one group responsible for risk management and one or more groups responsible for customer acquisition. Objectively, these groups are in direct conflict. To minimize risk, all a bank needs to do is to set acceptable risk thresholds as low as possible. This would minimize defaults and significantly improve profitability across all products. However, doing so would usually severely impact market growth and share value—in avoiding *all* risk, the bank would forgo customers who, while risky, might never default. This would also put their customer growth rates lower than the market average.

In this model, each group is responsible for a different outcome. The risk group is responsible for measuring and managing portfolio risk while the customer acquisition team is responsible for ensuring competitive or market-leading customer growth volumes. While distinct, these outcomes are interrelated. And by maintaining this conflict, the bank's leadership team can ensure they have access to equally valid (if different) points of view when making decisions.

These different points of view help create tension. They also help sow discord; more than one organization has collapsed into a collection of holding companies or personal fiefdoms because of it. While some tension encourages creativity and debate, too much creates a dysfunctional culture. The trick to tempering this tension is to create de facto diplomats, knowledgeable about the organization's broader context and capable of balancing the otherwise-polar positions these groups will sometimes take. While not usually an explicit part of their job description, their diplomacy comes through a combination of colocation and professional mobility.

Rather than being tied solely to one of the three groups, they move between them on a relatively regular basis, gaining exposure to all aspects of the business. Not only does this help temper political differences but it helps develop their understanding of the business, building their domain competencies and encouraging career progression and retention through exposure to new opportunities. To build trust and understanding, they work alongside their peers while in a particular group. Instead of being a disembodied voice on the other end of a phone, they become part of the team.

Because their skills are portable between business problems, data scientists and value architects fit this model perfectly. While they may still report into a different area, they become embedded in one of the three groups and help support invention, evolutionary improvements, or revolutionary innovation.

Finally, the prototype solutions that each of these groups develop need to be commercialized in some way. This may involve the operational use of their analytical assets such as the use of algorithms to guide product recommendations, such as Amazon's "Related to Items You've Viewed" or Netflix's Recommendations. It may involve the commercialization and/or productization of an algorithm such as the use of Quality Score by Google to inform AdWords. Commercialization goes beyond algorithms and mathematics. Among other things, it needs to meet regulatory and legal requirements. It needs to be robust and scalable enough to ensure business continuity. And, it needs to meet market requirements; a great idea is worthless if no-one is interested in it or if it's too expensive.

THE INNOVATION ENGINE

Eating the metaphorical elephant is easy. You just do it one mouthful at a time. It's the same in facilitating innovation; get the culture, structure, and focus right and magic happens.

Building the right structure starts with defining what it is you're trying to achieve and what the focus should be. Data can enable invention, making real a good idea. It can enable evolutionary innovation, delivering value through incremental improvements. It can also support revolutionary innovation, reinventing business models, and changing markets.

To succeed, groups need parameters to work within. Working off a totally blank page is exceedingly challenging; without knowing what success looks like, it's impossible to know when one's succeeded. The hunt for value from big data and business analytics can take place at two levels. Groups can search for local improvements in a targeted domain, using a business focus as the primary driver for direction. This equates to "going deep," diving into a particular area and exhaustively pursuing total process control and analytical perfection in a specific area. Examples include excellence in logistics, customer engagement, or pricing.

They can also search globally, looking to leverage a functional capability across many domains. This equates to "going broad," taking an existing analytical competency and exhaustively applying it across as

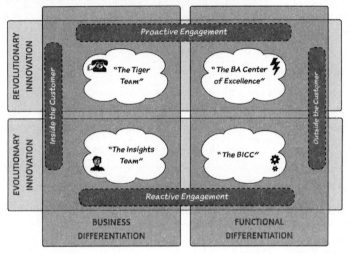

Figure 8.3 The Innovation Engine

many relevant business problems as they can find. An example might be reusing predictive modeling and operational analytics capabilities across customer retention, fraud prevention, and next-best-offer recommendations. Together, these give the *innovation engine*, as shown in Figure 8.3.

On the bottom half of the figure are groups focused on supporting stakeholders in solving known problems across the business. These often include "insights" groups, embedded analysts, and competency centers. Their main motivation is to deliver efficiency and continuous improvement through evolutionary innovations, honing their skills, and improving the performance engine. They tend to operate on a reactive basis, working in partnership with the business through a service-delivery model. They operate on an open-door policy, tightly integrated with business-as-usual operations.

In the top half are groups focused on finding the "unknown unknowns." These often include SWAT and Tiger teams as well as Centers of Excellence. Their main motivation is to identify and deliver change through revolutionary innovations, challenging the performance engine and chasing reinvention. They tend to operate on a proactive basis, actively hunting for opportunities to leverage big data and apply business analytics. Rather than waiting to be engaged, they talk in terms of value creation and look to drive organizational transformation.

On the left side of the figure are groups that usually exist inside their customers, being part of the group that covers their costs. Their focus is defined by their reporting line and their activities are often limited to a specific domain. Vertically focused, they align against a specific business function. Common examples include marketing analytics, logistical optimization, or pricing improvement.

On the right side are groups that usually exist outside their customers, usually operating as an organizational group function. Their focus is defined by their functional capabilities and their activities are directed toward problems that can be solved by their area of expertise. Horizontally aligned, they provide common functions to the broader organization. Common examples include business intelligence competency centers and analytical centers of excellence.

Their broader engagement means that they normally report to a group function. Groups in the bottom-right quadrant typically have a close alignment to IT service delivery and as such often report to the chief information officer or chief knowledge officer. Typically cost centers, they often operate as either a fixed-cost group or a combination fixed-cost or transfer-price group funded by project investment. Methodologies such as ITIL and other service-based, highly repeatable techniques work well—as their goal is usually repeatability and efficiency, they excel in delivering incremental value through operational efficiency.

Groups in the top right of the figure tend to emphasize flexibility and change. Their main requirement is to be located outside of their customers. When a group charged with enterprise transformation is located inside one of their customers, they regress to functional solutions and move from the right-hand side to the left-hand side of the framework. Equally, while there are examples where highly effective teams report to the chief information officer, their need for flexibility and fixed-cost-based exploration during the early stages of the innovation operating model tends to run counter to highly efficient

IT organizations. Because of this, common locations include reporting to the chief operating officer, the chief analytics officer, or the chief data scientist. There's nothing that precludes their existing under a group function such as the chief financial officer *as long as* they have a clear mandate to work across the group, not just in their own patch.

Success for these groups is usually measured by their ability to deliver value creation through change. Often operating as profit centers, whether through a direct profit and loss (P&L) or a shadow P&L, their goal is direct revenue generation, often to the point where the group is self-funded.

Groups in the bottom half of Figure 8.3 rarely require dedicated data scientists or value architects. Instead, their value comes from scale, repeatability, and service delivery. Groups in the top half, however, require data scientists and value architects if they are to succeed. Their value comes from reinvention and change. Without a clear linkage to value, the organization will typically reject the change they recommend.

A critical point about this framework is that a sufficiently large organization may have groups operating in all these quadrants. Rather than being a negative, this is actually a positive. Giving analysts the opportunity to see and solve both functional and enterprise business opportunities helps improve their "knowhow" and "understanding" dimensions within the human capital model described in Chapter 7. Giving them exposure to the variety of pressures each business unit faces helps improve their ability to act as a data diplomat, building their value architect skills and tempering tension without having to sacrifice the creativity it provides.

The aligning force behind what would otherwise be a highly complex and potentially conflicting model is the commercialization team sitting behind the scenes. As each group is responsible only for up to the prototyping stage, the commercialization group acts as a gate to ensure that big data and business analytics solutions are not needlessly duplicated. A defined and clear operating model helps ensure every group understands their role within the overall process and, given appropriate leadership, minimizes effort duplication.

Overall, this may seem complex. Unfortunately, so is the field. At its simplest, the answer is this: separate improvement from disruption and get the right teams focused on the right areas. Delivering a package from anywhere to anywhere else in the world overnight would once have seemed impossible. And yet, today we do it daily without a second thought. Get the model right and everything follows.

REINVENTING THE RŌNIN

An organization designed to facilitate innovation will have little success without the right people and culture. While the rōnin may have the skills needed to help generate value from big data, they won't always have the right mindset. The final piece of the picture is in getting people to *enable* the organization rather than *support* it; democratize analytics and anything's possible.

Getting the right person is only the start—once hired, they have the responsibility to use their skills to improve outcomes. Over time these responsibilities have changed, and not always in ways that fall within people's comfort zones. Consistent with the trends already discussed, the biggest of these changes has been a movement away from insight generation to driving change. This is more than just lip service—it requires very different responsibilities. Being aware of these differences and actively fostering them is one of the major differences between organizations that are successful in business analytics compared to those that are simply mediocre.

Much like how Henry Ford redefined manufacturing, the traditional approach is very focused on activities and delivery. Those who have highly technical and specialized skills play the role of an expert, driving insight and answering questions. Because their skills are scarce, they form the core of a larger team focused on generating insight. Their role within this team is to apply advanced analytics to create some form of insight. Once they have this insight, the rest of the team carries the responsibility to translate it into something that's easily digestible. This goes by many names but is often called a *presentation layer* and is delivered by the business intelligence (BI) team.

This information is then consumed by decision makers, usually with no linkage between the information and the resulting outcomes. Because decision making happens independently from reviewing insights, it's impossible to quantify how much of a difference the insight made in driving a better outcome. Planners may or may not review the reports produced by the BI team; even if they do read them, there's no guarantee that they acted on the insights.

Despite these limitations, this sequential approach makes intuitive sense. A core set of individuals extracts value, a larger set of individuals converts this intermediate good into a finished good, and the rest of the organization consumes that finished good. Henry Ford would be proud—the engineers do the work, the factory creates the product, and the public consumes the product. However, business analytics isn't manufacturing. As logical as it may be, it inevitably creates a number of insurmountable bottlenecks that demand a different approach.

The first and biggest bottleneck is that there are only so many people one can hire for this core group. Business analytics drives competitive differentiation and one of its biggest sources of value is its ability to solve multiple business problems at relatively low incremental cost. Most of the cost lies in acquiring the right skills, technology, process, and information—once these are in place, the organization capitalizes on economies of scope. Unfortunately, this still requires some degree of incremental resource. Because these skills are so scarce, it's extremely difficult to scale to solve other problems within the organization. Simply put, there aren't enough hours in the day to use this core team to solve other problems.

Paradoxically, this constraint isn't for technical reasons. One would intuitively think that because of the high degree of specialization required to understand many fields of advanced analytics, many of the barriers would be due to the tools used. This isn't the case— while sophisticated analytics requires deeply technical knowledge to apply safely and robustly, the tools themselves are becoming increasingly simple to use. Where building a predictive model used to require programming skills, modern tools allow someone with 20 minutes worth of training to develop a model. It may not necessarily be a good or robust model, but it will be a model and it will produce a prediction that in many cases is better than a guess.

Technologically, there is no good reason why everyone in the organization couldn't create their own insights. This concept is often referred to as the "democratization of analytics"—it revolves around giving everyone the freedom to develop their own insights.

Conceptually, this seems to eliminate the problem—if everyone can apply sophisticated analytics, specialized skills are irrelevant.

As with all oversimplifications, the reality is drastically different. It's important to remember that just because it's technically possible doesn't mean that it will produce a good outcome—knowledge, training, and experience are critical elements in producing a reliable prediction. Not all insights are equal and much of that specialist knowledge revolves around being able to differentiate reliable insights from those that are just mathematically attractive. As a very crude analogy, there's nothing to stop one claiming anything they want as a business expense on their personal income tax. Unfortunately, the immutable force of reality (the taxation office in this case) will normally provide a rather sobering experience if those questionable insights are acted on. Without a tax accountant's insights, it's dangerously easy to make some serious mistakes.

This specialization combined with a lack of technologically based constraints changes the operating model. Rather than being an analyst, the most advanced practitioners need to instead become mentors and quality control experts, providing overarching governance and guidance to those creating insight. Their role shifts from being the engine of analytics to being an enabler, becoming the fuel that helps drive innovation. The BI team, in turn, shifts from visualizing already-processed information to covering a broader spectrum of business analytics, usually covering both historical and predictive analytics. This is akin to becoming a "creator" of business analytics rather than just a "reporter." To prevent bad assumptions, the core mentoring team provides a level of governance and review over insights before they go into production.

This transformation continues to the "information consumers" who become "active decision makers." The distinction seems small but is enormous in practice—by linking the insights they've used to the outcomes and actions they've taken, they quantify the real value of business analytics. This is more than just a conceptual linkage and usually occurs at a very operational level with measurable differences. Reports gradually give way to workflows and approval processes.

Managing these newly defined skills takes focus; standard key performance indicators and management models rarely drive the most value. Organizations following a manufacturing approach tend to benchmark performance based on processing volumes, efficiency, and knowledge. There's good reason for this—they view analytics as a series of discrete activities. Their focus is usually on trying to integrate different business units, each of which often acts seemingly independently. Modelers are assessed on their ability to develop and deploy models. BI specialists are benchmarked on their ability to generate reports and insights are usually (but not always) designed to meet functional requirements defined by the business. Roles are normally defined based on technical knowledge.

One of the reasons this approach is so prevalent is because teams are usually arbitrarily defined based on technical skills. Rather than focusing on outcomes, an artificial distinction is made between the business intelligence or reporting team (often embedded within IT or finance), the analytics team (usually embedded within a functional line of business), and "the business." Because these groups are functionally and structurally separated, it makes sense to define roles in these terms. One of the biggest problems with this approach is that it makes it very difficult to task individuals based on outcomes—because technical activities and business outcomes are functionally separated, it's hard for the organization to link a group or individual's actions to specific outcomes.

Organizations focused on enablement usually benchmark performance on outcomes. Analytics is seen as being part of a value chain and not an activity in its own right. Management focus is usually on achieving economies of scope by solving multiple business problems across different functional areas. Mentors and creators are benchmarked not only on their ability to drive positive outcomes but also their ability to proactively drive value creation by engaging with decision makers. Roles are defined based on experience and competency (rather than the ability to use a particular piece of technology).

The benefits of this approach are enormous. First, the organization takes active steps toward achieving economies of scope by breaking down the barriers normally associated with functionally separated business units. Second, the organization overcomes many of the challenges inherent in hiring from a relatively small resource pool. Finally, it greatly simplifies measuring success—rather than make a subjective assessment of the value added by business analytics, it directly tracks outcomes through well-defined value chains. While it's still possible to realize value from business analytics without moving to an enablement model, adopting this approach helps drive maturity and competitive differentiation.

NOTES

1. Clayton M. Christensen, *The Innovator's Dilemma: When New Technologies Cause Great Firms to Fail* (Boston: Harvard Business School, 1997).
2. For more detail on how business analytics augments business models and leads to competitive differentiation, see Evan Stubbs, *Delivering Business Analytics: Practical Guidelines for Best Practice* (Hoboken, NJ: John Wiley & Sons, 2013), Chapter 2, and Evan Stubbs, *The Value of Business Analytics: Identifying the Path to Profitability* (Hoboken, NJ: John Wiley & Sons, 2011).
3. Vijay Govindarajan and Chris Trimble, *The Other Side of Innovation: Solving the Execution Challenge* (Boston: Harvard Business School, 2010).
4. James K. Esser, "Alive and Well after 25 Years: A Review of Groupthink Research," *Organizational Behavior and Human Decision Processes* 73, nos. 2–3 (1998): 116–141.

CHAPTER **9**

Creating a Plan

Without knowing where you want to go, it's impossible to know where you'll end up. However, it's important to remember that a plan is just a plan. Paraphrasing one of the world's greatest military strategists, Helmuth von Moltke the Elder, "No plan survives beyond first contact." Spending months of effort and millions of dollars on internal costs and consultants to develop the "perfect" strategy is an instant recipe for disaster.

STARTING THE CONVERSATION

The best approach is to start and finish with a vision. From there, learn by doing, not by theorizing. Large-scale change is both risky *and* uncertain, especially when it comes to culture. Without the ability to point to clear successes on the way, even the best attempts to create a new culture will fail. Because of this, business analytics and innovation from big data are best supported through continual incremental returns rather than all-encompassing programs of work. Success comes from building plans that involve shorter time to return, plans that rely heavily on experimentation and continual feedback, and plans that emphasize delivery over creativity. Always keep in mind that the most innovative solutions in the world are worthless if they can't be commercialized.

Successful leadership requires three things:

1. Knowing where you're going
2. Bringing everyone with you
3. Making others equally responsible for the journey

It's essential to remember that business analytics is a team sport focused on cultural change, first and foremost. Because of this, planning *must* be designed to form a team. Without this coalition of the willing, the best attempts will fail; when the team disappears, business analytics devolves into analytics.

Knowing where you want to go is essential. Somewhat surprisingly, working out the precise path to get there is less important. Few journeys follow the planned route exactly. Instead, most journeys take a variety of detours along the way, visiting interesting destinations while still moving in the right general direction.

Because of the rapid rate of change in big data and business analytics, plans should follow a similar philosophy. In the early stages opportunism should be the focus, working off a maximum 12-month return cycle. Any innovations or proposed projects that take longer than a 12-month delivery cycle should be de-prioritized in favor of opportunities with shorter return cycles. There's nothing wrong with extending this horizon as incremental successes help build trust. What's important is *getting* there, not planning for it.

The remainder of this part of the text runs through a few planning tools that may help move a group through the storming, norming, and forming stages of team creation.[1] They provide an example framework from which a leader can expand, covering:

- Defining a vision through the use of the *Cover Story*
- Identifying opportunities through the use of an *Affinity Map*
- Mapping responsibilities through the use of a *Stakeholder Matrix*

When executed effectively, they can help bring a group together, establish a common vision, and start working out individual responsibilities.

DEFINING THE VISION

This exercise helps the team create a view of what the future could look like. This vision will act as a framework to start developing a change plan leveraging big data and business analytics. It will act as a mobilizing force to consolidate the core team and allow everyone to state a common vision and message. And, it will act as a litmus test against which initiatives can be examined to confirm that they will move the organization in the right direction.

As the facilitator, by the end of this exercise your group should have:

- A variety of potential "constraint-free" future states for the organization or business unit
- A point from which to start working backward to develop potential initiatives and opportunities

The full exercise should take approximately 1 to 1.5 hours.

Approach

The goal of the exercise is to get the team to develop of a vision of how big data and business analytics might transform the organization. Once this vision is agreed, it's simply a case of mapping out everything that would need to be in place to make it a reality.

There are often two challenges in trying to create a strategy for innovation from big data. First, it's a technical field. People often feel uncomfortable strategizing in a domain they may know little about. What happens in most cases is that the technocrats direct the conversation while the business experts stay quiet.

Second, it's steeped in detail. Reality often acts as an anchor, constraining our creativity. Rather than think of the way things *could* be, individuals will often think about how things are and how things might incrementally change. When this happens, strategic planning turns into tactical planning and the team focuses almost exclusively on evolutionary innovations.

Mitigating these challenges is straightforward. Rather than plan around technology, the plans should always be defined in the context of the business. What's important are the *business* and *value* outcomes, not the *technical* outcomes. For example, many teams immediately leap to their organization becoming a "leader in big data." Unfortunately, this is largely meaningless and probably very expensive. Creating infrastructure just to be better than everyone else does little to improve profitability or shareholder value.

Instead, the team might focus on what that might mean for the organization's customers. In most cases, it's unlikely that any particular customer will care what kind of infrastructure the organization is using behind the scenes. However, having access to broad and deep behavioral information might enable new forms of offer relevancy. It might eliminate the need for all physical branches, moving to a totally virtual engagement structure.

As the facilitator, the goal is to get the team to think as creatively as they can and then get them to take it one step further. Rather than focus solely on evolutionary or revolutionary innovations, the facilitator should be guiding the team to think harder in the areas where they're not necessarily focusing. Think not only within your industry vertical but across industries as well; where might you expand into new businesses? How might your business model change and what might that mean for how the organization is currently structured?

However, this still needs to be somewhat grounded in reality; the team needs to understand that the final vision should represent an aspirational, game-changing position for the company in question. It's not an exercise in science-fiction. Suggestions about inventing telepathic devices should be qualified based on how feasible they are.

Equally, specificity is important—generalities like "right offer at the right time" should be probed and clarified. What does that mean in practice? How do those offers go out? How might they change the customer's relationship with the organization?

And finally, not everything need focus solely on big data or business analytics. *All* good ideas should be captured. Big data and business analytics are a core part of business but they're not the only part.

Instructions

Using the Cover Story template shown in Figure 9.1, get the groups to create the story of your organization 10 years from today, told "after the fact." The story should have narrative; it needs to be

Figure 9.1 The Cover Story

interesting enough that it would justify being on the cover of one or more magazines.

Each group should structure their narrative around the following sections:

- **Cover:** Describes the major success achieved by the organization or business unit. It should be a one-liner, suitable for the magazine or publication's cover. To help the group ideate, get them to consider what might be significant enough that the magazines they've identified would dedicate an entire issue to their organization.

- **Headlines:** Outlines the detail behind the story in headline form. These should also be one-liners and would represent the articles contained within the special edition or focus issue.

- **Sidebars:** Interesting side stories associated with the major success. While somewhat tangential, they should fill out the edges of the narrative.

- **Quotes:** Quotes from people involved, benefiting from, or impacted by, the success (inside or outside the organization). These should be written from the perspective of the individual being described, not from the perspective of a marketer. In many cases, it helps to do a sanity check on whether someone might actually say the quote in question.

The groups should also identify which magazines are publishing the material they describe. Is it *Time* magazine, *U.S. Banker*, a special edition of *The Economist*? To get the most out of the exercise, the facilitator should employ the following approach:

- Split the team into two groups of maximum six people. If there are too many people, split them into equal groups of no more than six people.

- Each group gets its own markers, templates, and sticky notes and is responsible for populating the template.

- Allow everyone 5 minutes to consider their own view of what the future might look like.

- At the end of the 5 minutes, each group should work collaboratively to generate one common story over the next 30–45 minutes. The goal is to create a strong narrative, working from the end-state back to today. What's important are the results and outcomes, not the details on *how* they got there.

- At the end of the collaboration session, each group then has 5–10 minutes to present their findings.

- Once each group has presented, the team should discuss common themes, observations, insights, or concerns about what each of the future states might imply.

- The team should then work together to create a single common vision.

IDENTIFYING OPPORTUNITIES

This exercise helps the team use the overarching vision to define potential points of improvement through structured brainstorming. It focuses on the future and ignores existing organizational constraints; the goal is to map out what would need to be put in place to achieve the vision.

As the facilitator, by the end of this exercise your group should have:

- A series of potential improvements or opportunities aligned by functional, outcome, or domain groupings

- A starting point for prioritizing projects or programs of work based on potential value

The full exercise should take approximately 30 minutes to 1.5 hours.

Approach

The goal of the exercise is to get the team to work out what's needed to achieve the vision. It might be technology. It might be new skills. It might even be a significant change in culture. It will probably need all of these along with many other things.

By identifying the necessary building blocks and grouping them into categories, the team will often find patterns that map fairly cleanly into logical programs of work. The more information and the better the clustering from the exercise, the more valuable the output. As the facilitator, feel free to get engaged to ensure an appropriate level of granularity and parsimony.

Instructions

Starting with the vision established through the Cover Story exercise, complete the Affinity Map template shown in Figure 9.2.

- Spend 10 minutes having each participant write sticky notes on how the organization could move toward achieving the vision. It might help to frame these around what new capabilities might be needed across people, process, data, and technology. If the vision involves real-time customer engagement and the organization doesn't yet have a real-time

Figure 9.2 Affinity Map

communications platform, then that would justify a sticky note. If there's broad reluctance to doing things differently, there might need to be a more customer-centric culture. The goal is to generate as many as possible; feel free to inject a bit of competition to reward whoever gets the most sticky notes up on the wall.

- At the end of this period, paste these sticky notes on the wall and, based on consensus and discussion, group them into categories. These categories should be organically determined and iteratively allocated, striking a balance between excessive granularity and oversummarization. They might span function, outcome, domain, or activity—as long as the groupings are internally consistent, they're doing their job. For context, these categories will eventually form the basis for identifying the streams of work that will need to be put in place to achieve the vision. Put any sticky notes that don't immediately fit into the "parking lot" for further consideration or discussion.

- Avoid spending time discussing categories—if there is overlap and disagreement, write both and consider consolidating them if some categories are underrepresented. Aim to achieve a large number of data points with a reasonably parsimonious set of categories. These categories should represent initiatives that *could* feasibly be delivered in under a year. If they would take longer than a year to deliver, consider how the initiative might be broken into smaller chunks of work.

- Once categorized, the team should then group the initiatives into logical phases. External value and ease of execution should be the focus; quick wins should be early.

MAPPING RESPONSIBILITIES

This exercise helps the team plan the core of an engagement strategy. It uses the outputs from the prior exercise as the guiding framework and identifies key influencers, decision makers, and other stakeholders of interest. The goal is to work out who should be included in the planning process and how they should be engaged.

As the facilitator, by the end of this exercise your group should have:

- A ranked list of key stakeholders across the organization taking into account their influence and power
- A skeleton targeting plan for use within a broader communication plan
- A responsibility matrix that outlines each individual or group's engagement model

The full exercise should take approximately 1 to 2 hours.

Approach

The goal of the exercise is to get the team to start planning their communication and engagement strategy. Business analytics is primarily about change management; without getting broader organizational buy-in and commitment, even the best ideas will likely be rejected.

However, the reality is that not everyone has equal influence. Effective change management is more about identifying the *right* people to engage with rather than trying to influence *everyone*. There are usually more people that *could* be engaged than there are hours in the day and spending too much time on communication can actually be detrimental. Communication is important. So is delivery.

It's useful to view things in terms of interest and influence. Those who have low influence on the vision may simply need to be kept occasionally informed, ideally through low-touch techniques such as quarterly briefings. Those who have high influence on the vision but low interest may need regular catchups along with a strong value proposition to get them enthused. Those who have low influence but high interest might be the ideal people to join the coalition of the willing, becoming change agents in their own right. And, those who have high influence and high interest may make ideal sponsors or champions to take part or full ownership over aspects of the transformation.

Instructions

Using the Stakeholder Analysis template shown in Figure 9.3, list and map as many stakeholders as possible who will be impacted by, can influence, or will make decisions on the shortlisted target initiatives.

- Using sticky notes, populate the Stakeholder Analysis template with key stakeholders. Have the team populate the template with only the people who are directly relevant to phase 1 of the vision *as well as* people who have influence over key stakeholders to the vision. The goal is not to create a comprehensive organization chart; be pragmatic.

- As the sticky notes are attached to the template, pay specific attention to their relative power: the ability to make or break a project does not always map to seniority or formal responsibility. If everyone clusters around a particular quadrant, rescale the entire diagram—not everyone has the same level of influence.

- Once completed, review the relative position of everyone and discuss how or where people's interests may not align to the targeted state. Where their current reality does not match the state that the vision would require, discuss what might influence their position.

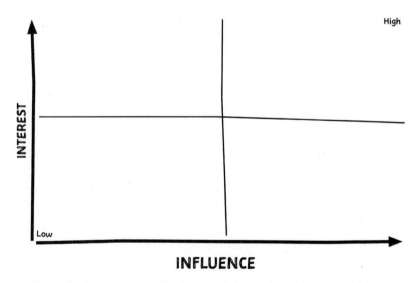

Figure 9.3 The Stakeholder Matrix

- Once the diagram has been finalized and the group agrees on everyone's relative positioning, tag each person with a *RACI* code representing the targeted communication model. Each stakeholder should have at least one letter written on their sticky note along with the initiative it refers to (identified in the previous exercise). If they will need to be *responsible* for the initiative, they should have an *R*. If they will need to *assist* but won't be responsible, they should have an *A*. If they have valuable insight and should be *consulted*, they should have a *C*. Finally, if they should simply be kept *informed*, they should have an *I*.

- The team should then go through each of the initiatives identified within phase 1 from the previous exercise and continue to map them against all the stakeholders in the influence map. Once completed, the data can be entered into a spreadsheet and expanded into a comprehensive communications and engagement strategy.

TAKING IT TO THE NEXT LEVEL

These exercises serve as an excellent starting point. There's nothing to stop an adroit leader from extending them; other useful exercises might include:

- Working out how best to link activities to value through a common measurement framework
- Creating a roadmap of initiatives that balance internal and external value
- Crowdsourcing innovative through participative innovative
- Turbocharging innovation through hackathons or other competitive games

Remember: the goal is not just to innovate. It's also to have fun.

NOTE

1. Using visual techniques is an excellent way of getting people engaged. Good books on the subject include David Sibbet, *Visual Leaders: New Tools for Visioning, Management, & Organization Change* (Hoboken, NJ: John Wiley & Sons, 2013), and Luke Hohmann, *Innovation Games: Creating Breakthrough Products through Collaborative Play* (Boston: Addison-Wesley, 2007).

Conclusion: The Final Chapter Is Up to You

There's not much more to say. Those who have the responsibility and power to act on the information provided in this book should count themselves lucky; it's not often that one gets the opportunity for reinvention.

Whether this book made the uncertain clear or simply validated what you already knew, the question is what you'll do with this knowledge. Ideas are cheap; action, on the other hand, is hard.

Make a plan. Work out who has the interest and influence to also make the change. Create a vision and make it real. Transform the world.

The final chapter is up to you.

We live in interesting times; I hope that together we make the world even more interesting.

Glossary

Advanced Analytics
A subset of analytical techniques that, among other things, often uses statistical methods to identify and quantify the influence and significant of relationships between items of interest, group similar items together, create predictions, and identify mathematical optimal or near-optimal answers to business problems.

Agent-Based Modeling
A computationally driven modeling approach that simulates the local interactions of autonomous agents with the goal of monitoring global outcomes.

Aggregation
A process by which variables are summed based on a classification or temporal hierarchy. Common examples include totaling all sales for a given time period or geographic region.

Algorithm
A finite series of well-defined steps that achieve a desired outcome. These steps may be deterministic or include random or probabilistic elements.

Analytics
A data-driven process that creates insight. These processes incorporate a wide variety of techniques and may include manual analysis, reporting, predictive models, time series models, or optimization models.

Analytics Platform
A technology platform that provides standardized tools, an ability to collaborate, and the ability to migrate insight into operational processes.

Assets
Items of economic value created by a team through the application of competencies and tools. Within a business analytics context they are normally intangible in nature and often include models, processes, and electronic documentation.

Big Data
A colloquial term referring to datasets that are otherwise unwieldy to deal with in a reasonable amount of time in the absence of specialized tools. Common characteristics include large amounts of data (volume), different types of data (variety), and ever-increasing speed of generation (velocity). They typically require unique approaches for capture, processing, analysis, search, and visualization.

Business Analytics
The process of leveraging all forms of analytics to achieve business outcomes through requiring business relevancy, actionable insight, and performance management and value measurement. These business outcomes are typically tangible and/or intangible value of interest to the organization.

Business Intelligence
A broad classification of information systems–based technologies that support the identification and presentation of insight. Common historical usage referred primarily to reporting-focused systems, but usage of the term has been broadened by some to include all forms of insight generation (including exploratory data analysis and predictive analytics).

Business Planning
An intermediate level of strategic planning, typically focusing on the individual strategies that will lead to the broader organizational strategies. It may include the creation of competitive differentiation, cost minimization, or vertical integration.

Center of Excellence
A centralized group targeted with supporting *and* driving change across the organization. Focus areas often vary based on organizational strategy and vision.

Champion/Challenger Process
A process that benchmarks alternative processes against the currently selected process. If an alternative, challenger process outperforms the current, champion process, the champion process is usually replaced with the challenger process.

Churn
A term that refers to a customer going to a different provider. Depending on the context, it may refer to a total migration away from the organization in question through to a reduction in consumption.

Community of Practice
An often virtual group intended to distribute knowledge, share experience, and cross-pollinate best practices across the organization.

Competencies
Reusable and generalizable skills held by a business analytics team. One common example is the ability to build predictive models.

Competency Center
A centralized group targeted with supporting the organization in particular competency. Focus areas often vary based on organizational strategy and vision.

Competitive Advantage
A strategic advantage held by one organization that cannot be matched by its competitors. This advantage may or may not be sustainable and, if not, may eventually be replicated by its competitors.

Contagious Churn/Viral Churn
A situation where individuals cancel their service because people in their network have canceled their service. Common reasons include being made aware of better options and "pull-through" by leveraging positive network externalities.

Cross-Sectional Modeling
A variety of methods that focus on analyzing time captured across entities at a specific point in time. Common applications include identifying differences between groups, relationships between outcomes and causal factors, and creating predictions.

Cross-Sell
A process by which new, nonoverlapping products are sold to existing customers.

Crowdsourcing
The process by which ideas, services, or other needs are solicited from predominantly amorphous and undefined large groups of people.

Data Cleansing
The process of detecting, removing, or correcting incorrect data.

Data Management Process
A series of well-defined steps that take source data, conduct a series of operations on it, and deliver it to a predefined location.

Datamart
A shared repository of data, often used to support functional areas within the business. It is sometimes used as the direct access layer to the data warehouse.

Data Quality
A broad term that refers to the accuracy and precision of data being examined. Data that exhibits high quality correctly quantifies the real-world items it represents.

Data Scientist
A person who blends deep analytical skills with a scientific mindset. They often have sufficient domain expertise to innovate or invent.

Data Warehouse
A shared repository of data, often used to support the centralized consolidation of information for decision support.

Decision Tree
An algorithm that focuses on maximizing group separation by iteratively splitting variables.

Derived Variable
A variable not included in the original data but based on the underlying characteristics of the source data. Common examples include calculating a three-month moving average and calculating Recency, Frequency, and Monetary statistics.

Departmental Platform
A centralized analytics environment based on a defined set of tools that supports a department or functional unit within an organization.

Design of Experiments
An experimentation process by which the impact of various influencers on items of interest can be tested in an efficient manner.

Discovery Environment
A logically defined and usually separate area within an analytics platform that provides users with the ability to create assets and generate insight.

Doge
A meme, often represented by a Shiba Inu: many views; much awesome.

Economies of Scale
The process by which cost per unit of output declines as production scales increase. A common driver is the presence of high fixed costs.

Economies of Scope
The process by which cost per unit of outputs declines as diversification increases.

Enabling Initiative
A business analytics initiative focused on creating processes or assets needed for a planned growth initiative or to deliver evolutionary efficiency improvements.

Enterprise Platform
A centralized analytics environment based on a defined set of tools that supports the entire organization.

Enterprise Resource Planning
A variety of software-based systems that aim to standardize processes and information management within organizations, typically focusing on operational processes, including finance and accounting, supply chain and logistics, inventory management, and resource management.

Evolutionary Innovation
Improvements that take an existing process or activity and make it better.

Fiber Channel
A high-speed networking standard often used for storage networks, running on both twisted-pair copper and fiber-optic.

Functional Planning
The most granular level of strategic planning, typically focusing on the operational activities needed to achieve the objectives outlined at the business level. It normally revolves around processes and resources and activities at this level are the most specific, often dealing with detailed execution plans and individual resources.

Future Shock
A term coined by Alvin Toffler in his book, *Future Shock*, first published in 1970. It describes the confusion and shattering psychological stress created from too much change over a relatively short period. Symptoms include distress and disorientation.

Grouping Model
A type of model specifically focuses on grouping similar individuals or entities together based on multidimensional information. A common example is a customer segmentation model.

Growth Initiative
A business analytics initiative focused on creating value. They tend to have fairly well-defined deliverables, and fixed timeframes with expected end-dates, and involve the creation of new assets and processes.

Hax and Wilde's Delta Model
A way of looking at competitive advantage that looks for ways of maximizing the customer value proposition to achieve maximal customer bonding. It describes three broad strategies: best product, total customer solutions, and system lock-in.

High-Context Culture
A grouping of individuals with a tendency to rely on cultural norms and implicit communication when communicating. Cultural history and understanding is often extremely important.

HiPPO
The Highest Paid Person's Opinion.

Ideation
The process of generating and communicating ideas. It includes the innovation process and should eventually lead to commercialization.

Impute
The process of estimating likely values for missing data taking into account the statistical characteristics of the broader population, often simultaneously trying to minimize the bias introduced through estimation.

In-Database Processing
A technique involving migrating logic processing away from a generalized computing tier and into the database. A common example in analytics is transforming analytical processing steps into native database execution logic and deploying this logic into the database.

Independent Variables
A term referring to the inputs used within a model. They are typically unrelated to one another but should exhibit some form of causal relationship toward the outcome being examined.

Information Asymmetries
A situation where one individual has an information advantage over another. It is typically a source of market failure and leads to pricing inefficiencies.

Innovation

The application of novel ideas to improve things that already exist. Sometimes, this different approach may be evolutionary. At other times, it may involve high amounts of disruption and be revolutionary.

Intangible Value

The immeasurable worth of an asset of outcome to an organization. Common examples include job satisfaction and the ability to make better decisions.

Invention

The original creation of a new thing based on a novel idea.

Join

Key Performance Indicator (KPI)A measure by which job performance is assessed. Often, bonuses or other rewards mechanisms are tied to these. See *Merge*.

Kryder's Law

The trend for magnetic disk storage to double annually, leading to significant ongoing increases in storage capacity. It was defined by Mark Kryder while at Seagate.

Low-Context Culture

A grouping of individuals with a tendency to explicitly communicate concepts and avoid relying on "things left unsaid." Cultural history and understanding tends to be less important.

Market Failure

An economic condition where the allocation of goods by the market creates an inefficient outcome. In the absence of intervention, the free market will achieve a suboptimal result. Common examples include the creation of negative market externalities such as pollution or the abuse of shared public grounds, commonly known as the "tragedy of the commons."

Meme

A term coined by Richard Dawkins, it describes an idea or other cultural element that replicates from individual to individual through nongenetic means.

Merge

A process by which two or more tables are combined into one, matching them using one or more common fields. A common example involves combining customer data with purchasing data to create a single table that incorporates all available information.

Micro-Segmentation Modeling
A segmentation approach that creates very high numbers of segments, often in the thousands.

Model
An abstracted view of reality. Within analytics, it often refers to a mathematically or logically defined function that helps simplify multidimensional information into a small set of useful measures.

Model Deployment
The process by which models are migrated from a discovery environment into an operational environment and used to provide ongoing scoring processes.

Model Development
The process by which models are created.

Model Factory
A service designed to support the rapid creation and execution of analytical methods. They often make heavy use of automation, templates, and other mass-production methods to achieve scale and efficiency that would otherwise be impossible.

Monte Carlo Sampling
A process by which samples are repeatedly drawn with replacement from an existing population. Typically, Monte Carlo sampling is used as an input generation process to run a variety of simulations and capture the resulting outputs.

Moore's Law
The trend for the number of transistors on an integrated circuit to double roughly every two years, leading to significant ongoing increases in computing power. It was defined by Gordon E. Moore, cofounder of Intel.

Multivariate Analysis
A form of statistical analysis that includes more than one variable at a time.

Organizational Benefits
Benefits that accrue to the broader organization.

Operational Activity
An ongoing process focused on preserving existing value. They tend to be more process-driven, have no fixed end date, and leverage existing assets, capabilities, and processes.

Operational Environment
A logically defined and usually separate area within an analytics platform that provides users with the ability to deploy assets into processes and workflows to support operational activities.

Operations Research
A subset of analytical techniques that apply mathematical optimization techniques to identify optimal or near-optimal answers to business problems. It is often used to support inventory optimization and supply-chain optimization, and optimize the allocation of scarce resources.

Opportunity Cost
The cost of the next-best choice to someone who has picked from a series of mutually exclusive options. It represents the option forgone.

Organizational Planning
The highest level of strategic planning, typically focusing on identifying the markets where the organization will or won't compete, targeting acquisitions or creating key competencies and cultures.

Performance Management
The application of technology, process, and psychology to manage behavior and results and facilitate the delivery of strategic and tactical objectives.

Personal Benefits
Benefits that accrue to individuals within the organization.

Petabyte
An SI-defined measure of data storage equal to 1,000 terabytes. For comparison, a single commercial single-sided dual-layer DVD can store up to 8.54 gigabytes.

Precrime
A term coined by author Philip K. Dick, it describes a group tasked with using prescience to identify and prevent crimes that have not yet occurred.

Predictive Modeling
A process by which the underlying relationships behind an outcome are identified, quantified, and used to create predictions for new information. These are often statistically based. A common example is using information about customers who have canceled their phone service to statistically identify and quantify the major leading indicators that suggest someone will cancel. These indicators are then translated into a scoring process and used to score existing customers, helping to identify those who are at a high probability of cancellation. Once identified, they can then be

contacted before they cancel, potentially making a unique retention offer to discourage them from going to a competitor.

Pricing Analytics
The application of analytics to specifically support calculating optimal prices and understand the relationship between prices and demand through price elasticity models.

Propensity Model
A type of model that specifically focuses on creating predictions around the likelihood of an individual doing a particular action. Common examples include the propensity to default on a loan or to purchase a given product.

Psychohistory
A term coined by Isaac Asimov, it describes the application of psychology, sociology, and applied statistics to make predictions about population-level future behaviors.

Radio-Frequency Identification (RFID)
A low-power technology that supports low-cost wireless communication between readers and devices. Because of its low-cost structures, it is used to support a wide variety of asset management problems ranging from tracking casino chips to monitoring usage of toll roads.

Ratemaking
A variety of techniques that specifically focus on calculating premiums taking into account the frequency and severity of loss-making events.

Recency, Frequency, Monetary Analysis (RFM)
A technique commonly used in marketing applications to profile customer spending patterns. It derives a series of variables to identify how recently each customer spent money, how frequently they spend money, and how much money they spend with the organization in question.

Relational Model
A type of model that aims to identify relationships of interest and quantify the strength of relationship between individuals or entities. Common examples include market basket analysis and social network analysis.

Reporting
A process by which insight is presented in a visually appealing and informative manner.

Revolutionary Innovation
Improvements that either create a new process or activity or take an existing process or activity and make it redundant.

Roadmap
Within the context of business analytics, a defined set of staged initiatives that deliver tactical returns while moving the team toward strategic outcomes.

Scoring Process
A process by which a predefined model is applied against new data, creating a new variable for each record that contains the result of the model. A common example is calculating the propensity of every customer to churn within a given time period.

Scoring Table
A table containing new data that is to be fed through a model converted to a scoring process, the output of which is usually a series of numerically based recommendations.

Segmentation
A process by which entities within a population are grouped into segments that have common characteristics. This grouping process may be manually, algorithmically, or statistically based and will often take into account anywhere from a handful to hundreds of common attributes across all the entities.

Segmentation Strategy
A strategy that identifies subgroups within the market and treats these groups differently. This targeted treatment can then drive offer relevancy and increase offer attractiveness.

Sensitivity Analysis
A form of simulation modeling that focuses specifically on identifying the upper and lower bounds of model outputs given a series of inputs with specific variance.

Sensor Data
Data generated by machines.

Simulation
A process by which processes or models are run repeatedly using a variety of inputs. The outputs are normally captured and analyzed to conduct sensitivity analysis, provide insight around likely potential outcomes, and identify bottlenecks and constraints within existing processes or models.

Simulation Modeling
An analytical technique that often involves running models repeatedly using a variety of inputs to determine the upper and lower bounds of possible outcomes. This simulation process is also sometimes used to identify the likely distribution of outputs given a series of assumptions around how the inputs are distributed.

Single View of Customer (SVoC)
A consolidated view of all customer information within an organization.

Smart Meter
Consumption data generated by electrical meters and sent back to the utility in set intervals, often every 15 minutes.

Social Network Analysis
The application of analytics to analyze relationships between individuals, often to help with contagious churn or viral marketing.

Six Sigma Process Improvement
A business management strategy focusing on quality control testing and optimizing processes through reducing process variance.

Strategic Planning
The process by which organizations identify a desired outcome, the resources required to support that outcome, and the plan to achieve the outcome. Typically, strategic planning is an important step in identifying the creation of new competitive advantages.

Stress Testing
A form of simulation modeling that focuses specifically on identifying the response of a model under specific, often highly negative scenarios. Common examples include testing the profitability of a bank given catastrophic levels of mortgage defaults or modeling extreme macroeconomic conditions.

Strongly Defined Process
A series of steps that is clearly defined, is repeatable, can be automated, and leads to the creation of value.

Structured Data
Data that fits cleanly into a predefined structure.

Tangible Value
The quantifiable and measurable worth of an asset or outcome to an organization. Common examples include financial improvements and saleable market value.

Team Platform
A centralized analytics environment based on a defined set of tools that supports a business analytics team.

Terabyte
An SI-defined measure of data store equal to 1,000 gigabytes. For comparison, a single commercial single-sided dual-layer DVD can store up to 8.54 gigabytes.

Time Series Analysis
A variety of methods that focus on analyzing time-stamped information, often with an emphasis on identifying relationships between events and outcomes as well as creating predictions.

Tools
The basic building block through which most assets are created. They can be internally developed or purchased off the shelf, but without an appropriate set of purpose-built tools, a business analytics team is unable to create any new assets.

Training Table
A table containing data that is to be used to develop a model.

Transformation
A mathematically defined way of taking data and altering it based on a generalized mapping function, often with the goal of creating a different way of looking at the data in an easily reversible way. Common examples include taking the natural logarithm or exponentiation.

Unstructured Data
Data that cannot fit cleanly into a predefined structure.

Upsell
A process by which customers are upgraded to more expensive products, replacing their existing products.

Value
The intrinsic and extrinsic worth of an asset or outcome to an individual or organization.

Value Architect
A person who blends change management skills with analytical knowledge. They often have sufficient practical experience and emotional intelligence to transform an organization into an analytical competitor.

Viral Marketing
The application of direct marketing with the goal of leveraging individual's personal networks to promote a message, increase mindshare, or drive pull-through sales through positive network externalities.

Weakly Defined Process
A series of steps that leads to the creation of value, is based on guidelines, and relies on the skill and ingenuity of the analyst to complete successfully.

About the Author

Evan Stubbs lives in Sydney, Australia, one of the few places in the world where a 30-hour flight itinerary fails to raise even a single eyebrow. His childhood was mainly spent (often unsuccessfully) avoiding brain-controlling parasites, civil war, and biblical floods. He now spends most of his spare time filling in bandicoot holes in his backyard, avoiding murderous redbacks, writing, and otherwise keeping life (somewhat less) interesting.

He's also the Chief Analytics Officer for SAS Australia/New Zealand and sits on the board of the Institute of Analytics Professionals of Australia. He's a prolific speaker and evangelist for the power of analytics. Over the years he's developed human–machine interfaces for concept cars, developed models that predict criminal behavior, and helped leadership teams navigate the upcoming storm.

Index